CROSSCURRENTS
PURSUING SOCIAL JUSTICE AND INTERRELIGIOUS WORK
SINCE 1950

CrossCurrents (ISSN 0011-1953; online ISSN 1939-3881) connects the wisdom of the heart with the life of the mind and the experiences of the body. The journal is operated through its parent organization, the Association for Public Religion and Intellectual Life (APRIL), an interreligious network of academics, activists, artists, and community leaders seeking to engage the many ways religion meets the public. Contributions to the journal exist at the nexus of religion, education, the arts, and social justice. The journal is published quarterly on behalf of the Association for Public Religion and Intellectual Life by the University of North Carolina Press.

The Association for Public Religion and Intellectual Life (formerly ARIL) is a global network of leaders, scholars, and social change agents who explore religious life, engage in intellectual inquiry, and lead ethical action in the world today. Their primary objective, especially through annual summer colloquia and *CrossCurrents*, is to bring together leading voices of our time to advocate for justice and to examine global spiritual and interreligious currents in both historical and contemporary perspectives.

A membership to APRIL includes access to *CrossCurrents* starting with Volume 58, 2008, though our partners at Project MUSE, monthly newsletters, early access to summer colloquium themes, a 40% on UNC Press books, and more. For more information, including membership and subscription rates, visit www.aprilonline.org.

This reissue of *CrossCurrents* was one of four issues published in 2020 as part of Volume 70. For a current masthead visit www.aprilonline.org.

© 2020 Association for Public Religion and Intellectual Life. All rights reserved.

ISBN 978-1-4696-6671-6 (Print)

CROSSCURRENTS

VOLUME 70, NO 4 ISSN 0011-1953

70TH ANNIVERSARY ISSUE
Edited by Charles Henderson

327
Love, Light, and Catholic Mysticism in Vincent van Gogh
Angelo Caranfa

349
Let Us Never Forget
Bob Blundell

354
Evangelizing a Modern Agnostic Culture
Eugene P. Trager

360
Gay Men, the Invention of Ecclesial Injustice, and Aspirations for Redress and Renewal
Joseph N. Goh

378
Washington Gladden and the Christian Nation
Alfredo Romagosa

394
Renouncing Harvard: The Ascetic Theology of Jonathan Tran
Thomas J. Millay

406
Mental Illness, The Second Amendment and Gun Violence
Eugene P. Trager

415
Book review: The Puritans: A Transatlantic History
Peter Heinegg

426
Book review: Religion As We Know It: An Origin Story
Peter Heinegg

427
Book review: An Emotional History of Doubt
Peter Heinegg

432
CrossCurrents at 48
Charles Henderson

446
A Brief History of the Research Colloquium
Charles Henderson

449
Contributors

About the Cover: Artwork on our anniversary issue cover was painted by Helene Masour.

CROSSCURRENTS

LOVE, LIGHT, AND CATHOLIC MYSTICISM IN VINCENT VAN GOGH

Angelo Caranfa

> Love is a mystery within a mystery.
>
> On the last day before ... the face of death, there was in [Socrates] something ... of a god, a ray of light from heaven.
>
> I just entered for a minute the Catholic Church where evening service was being held. It was a beautiful sight ... the church looked so cheerful in the evening light. – Vincent Van Gogh

Love and light in art as in mysticism

In *Love: A History*, Professor Simon May suggests that love is everywhere, writing: "Academic books, chat shows, pop lyrics, internet dating sites, self-help manuals—all buzz with curiosity about the conditions for successful love." After exploring the many philosophers and writers who have written on love, May concludes that "The nature of love—what exactly it is; what we demand from it—is sacred territory."[1] If Professor May had asked St. Teresa of Avila (1515-1582) whether love could be defined, he would have been mystified at the answer; because, unlike the figures he treats who seem to know what love is, St. Teresa believes that she is "not sure that [she] know[s] when love is spiritual and when there is sensuality mingled with it, or how to begin speaking about it."[2]

It is not until the nineteenth century—with the advance of science in all its aspects, natural, physical, mathematical, psychological, and social —that love loses its "sacred territory," and the tension between the "spiritual" and the "sensual" is broken. Today we speak of love or *erös* as though we "know" what it is: sexual desire, what Freud calls "libido," and Darwin associates it with the "selfish gene." But love involves real self-denuding that can propel us toward spiritual self-awakening, toward "sacred territory," toward completeness, toward a Presence. Mystics have long spoken of Presence as God within us and in the world. Perhaps

St. Augustine (354-430) says it best: "You were with me, and I was not with you."[3] In *The Varieties of Religious Experiences*, William James (1842-1910) cites from the life of Dr. Burke—a Canadian psychiatrist—to demonstrate a larger and a more fulfilling love than ordinary love, a love that leads to seeing the universe a living Presence:

> There came upon me a sense of exultation, of immense joyousness accompanied or immediately followed by an intellectual illumination impossible to describe.... I saw that the universe is not composed of dead matter, but is, on the contrary, a living Presence; I became conscious in myself of eternal life ... that the cosmic order is such that without any peradventure all things work together for the good of each and all; that the foundation principle of the world, of all the worlds, is what we call love.[4]

This love is thus an integral, generative, illuminating, and sustaining feature in the web of Life itself; it is the door to "eternal life," to a universe that is alive, Present, and that, according to St. John of the Cross (1542-1591), it is a gift of God's love, in which, consequently, even mountains, valleys, flowers, winds, and birds could sing the spiritual canticle of the Song of Songs.[5] The twentieth century Russian Orthodox theologian Nicolas Berdyaev (1879-1940) observes that this love is by its very nature creative. Hence it is "an ascent ... from the world to God. It moves ... towards eternity. The Products of creativeness remain in time, but the creative act itself, the creative flight, communes with eternity."[6] Hence the creative act, like the mystical experience, communes with eternity through love, real, sincere, true *erōs*: sacred, mystical, mysterious, enlightening, not reduced to pure sensuality, as it is today. Today some men see in a woman nothing, but flesh used for the satisfaction of his physical desires; his encounters with a woman is self-fulfilling rather than harmonizing, than enriching, than completing.

In the following pages I will concern myself with the theme of love and light in Vincent van Gogh (1853-1890) as it exhibits a parallel vision to Catholic mysticism. Although scholarship on van Gogh has focused on the religious aspect of his writings and art,[7] none relates his spiritual quest to Catholic mystical vision, none sees his sexual love as a paradigm for spiritual love, for a divine encounter, if only for a moment, with God's light. This study, however, does not make van Gogh a Catholic mystic—as Debora Silverman makes him a Buddhist monk, and in so doing she implies the dissolution of the self and of the world, which, in my opinion, is contrary to van Gogh's thoughts[8]—nor does van Gogh reflect the central doctrines of the Catholic faith. Rather, van Gogh does center himself upon the theme of love and light that reflects the Catholic spiritual tradition whose roots stretch back to Plato and Plotinus. After all, it is in the form of light that love invades us. St. Augustine writes: "I do love ... light.... [God] is the light.... Love knows ... that light.... He who knows that light knows eternity."[9]

Van Gogh reflects this Catholic vision of love and light. His words and art contain the darkness of humankind estranged from God as a result of the original sin and the *longing* to break through this darkness to the light of knowledge of God. Hence from the day we are born, says van Gogh, following St. Augustine, we walk, yes, we walk "from darkness to light."[10] This is the "light" of God that St. John of the Cross describes with an exquisite metaphor of the *Living Flame of Love*. In addition to love, light, and longing, Van Gogh also shares with Catholic mysticism the emphasis on the individual's inner self, and the vision of all creation as coming from and returning to God through the love of the beauty of creation. At the same time Catholic mystics place art in the service of ultimate theological mysteries in the Church as the *mystical body* of Christ; the hidden, the transcendent, the mystery, the spiritual, the sacramental, the incorporeal, and the self returning to God by love's ascent through knowledge. St. Catherine of Siena (1347-1380) writes: "She [Soul] has for some time ... become accustomed to dwelling in the cell of self-knowledge in order to know better God's goodness toward her, since upon knowledge follows love. And loving, she seeks to pursue truth and cloth herself in it."[11] By contrast, van Gogh stresses the personal, the visible, the imminent, the phenomenal, the natural, the secular, the corporeal, and the self returning to God by art as manifestation of the creative act. "A work [of art] that is good may not be eternal," observes van Gogh, "but the thought [love] expressed in it is" (*L*, 120). Hence van Gogh is a mystic of the sensual life of art, while the Catholic mystic is an artist of the spiritual life, yet both ascend toward Light itself through the use of symbols and images.[12]

The mystery of love intimately lived in life as in art

Van Gogh's biographical story of his love for Eugénie Loyer, Kee Vos, and Christine Clasina Maria Hoornik, known as Sien, is well known; as is his life of sexual dependency, of enjoying "the hour of the flesh."[13] What is less known is that what van Gogh seeks in his life is a real or an existential spirituality of love, a love intimately felt or experienced, which nevertheless remains a mystery: "What a mystery life is," van Gogh writes, "and love is a mystery within a mystery" (L, 265). Mysticism is about the mystery of life and of love. Van Gogh goes on to tell his brother Theo that true love "is like the discovery of a new hemisphere ... like a clear light in the night ... and it influences my work" (L, 154). Moreover, mysticism is creative; it is a journey of "discovery," of "light in the night." Of it St. John of the Cross observes: "For I know well the spring that / flows and runs, / Although it is night.... / Its clarity is never darkened, / And I know that every light has / come from it / Although it is night."[14]

In a similar vein, van Gogh confesses that, although it is "night" for him—the night of suffering, of inner conflicts, of failures, of anguish, of despair, of not knowing where he is and where he is going with his life—love, "the flame of God" within him, is not extinguished, but burns in him (L, 111). He writes: "I will seek ... Love, and go on beseeching the Spirit of God under all circumstances" (L, 82a). This is the Love that transforms van Gogh's sorrow into joy; and although he will fall many times, there will always remain in him a "longing for the heights away from the misery here below ... the longing of our hearts" (L, 82a) for the more we cannot see: "And if we feel ... that there is an eye looking down upon us, it would be well for us to lift up our eyes at times, as if to see the Invisible" (L, 112) or the Light or God himself who is Mystery. St. Catherine of Siena echoes what van Gogh says about longing; in fact, she sees "holy longing"[15] as a way to transcend one's self-knowledge and be passionately embraced by the invisible God.

Yet God makes himself visible in Christ, his only begotten Son "born of woman" (Gal 4:4) so that we may come to know the ineffable, unspeakable, and unknowable God. God becomes incarnate or human in Christ, the light that dispels all darkness, the love that redeems humankind after the original sin, and the beauty that renders God present in the world. Of the latter, Simone Weil (1929-1941) observes: "There is as it were an incarnation of God in the world and it is indicated by beauty. The beautiful is the experimental proof that the incarnation is possible. Hence all art of the highest order is religious in essence."[16] We should add that "all art of the highest order" flowers from the love the artist puts into the creation of beautiful images, stirring a yearning for the infinite, the eternal, the transcendent, the mystery, the holy, which van Gogh as a seeker of beauty express thus: "If one really loves nature, one can find beauty everywhere" (L, 16). This is the way St. Francis of Assisi (1181-1226) is transported to love God in all things, especially Brother Sun who "is beautiful and radiant with great splendor, / And bears the signification of you, Most High One."[17]

Unlike St. Francis, who is primarily inspired by Scripture as he contemplates the beauty of creation, van Gogh is inspired not only by the Scripture but by literary works as well, writing: "I have a more or less irresistible passion for books, and I continually want to instruct myself, to study if you like, just as much as I want to eat my bread" (L, 133). In fact, in a letter to his sister, Wilhelmina, van Gogh goes so far as to suggest that Scripture should be supplemented with literature, the "work of the French naturalists, Zola, Flaubert, Guy de Maupassant, de Goncourt," and asks, "Is the Bible enough for us?"[18] He continues: "In these days, I believe, Jesus himself would say to those who sit down in a state of melancholy ... get up and go forth. Why do you seek the living among the dead?" Yet van Gogh concludes the letter from a truly Franciscan perspective, writing:

> If the spoken or written word is to remain the light of the world, then it is our right and our duty to acknowledge that we are living in a period when it should be spoken and written in *such* a way that—in order to find something equally great, and equally good, and equally original, and equally powerful to revolutionize the whole of society—we may compare it with a clear conscience to the old revolution of the Christians (L, W1).

St. Francis too believed that if the written or spoken word of God "is to remain the light of the world," it should be preached or written in such a way that it is "good," "original," and "powerful." Hence one day, as he prayed in the deteriorating church of St. Damian outside Assisi, he heard a voice saying, "Francis, go and repair My house, which you see is falling down" and, by implication, to repair society as well.

Among the literary sources that instruct van Gogh are Dante (1265-1321), who "made an impression on me" (*L,* 539); Thomas à Kempis (1380-1471), whose *The Imitation of Christ* "can be compared to nothing else" (*L,* 267), and which "is sublime, and he who wrote it must have been a man after God's heart" (*L,* 108); John Bunyan (1628-1688), whose *Pilgrim's Progress* became the theme of his first sermon, "I am a stranger on the earth" (*L,* 31, 80, 82); Charles Dickens (1812-1870, whom van Gogh describes as "What an artist! There is no one like him" (*L,* 205); George Eliot (1819-1880), who moved van Gogh with her description of the life of the working class as the "'kingdom of God on earth,'" for these workers celebrate the Divine service "in a chapel in Lantern Yard" (*L,* 66); Jules Michelet (1798-1874), whose *L'Amour* was to van Gogh "both a revelation and a Gospel at the same time" (*L,* 20); Émile Zola (1840-1902), whose *La Joie de vivre* and *Une Page d'amour* he recommended to his sister, but which, together with the works of Michelet, he later told his brother to destroy (*L,* 39, 43).

What van Gogh draws from these and other literary sources[19] is a concept of love as a sublime, genuine, humble, simple, sincere, honest, intimate, gentle, pure, pious, compassionate, and deep *feeling* for things and for life itself in its personal and social aspects. In words that literally seem imported from *The Canticle of Brother Sun* of St. Francis of Assisi, Van Gogh tells his brother Theo that he should love everything that surrounds him; love a blade of grass, a dandelion, a hawthorn, a peach or an olive tree, a meadow, the sea, the sunset or the moon rising, the sky, the birds, the clouds, the whole of nature, where everything breathes serenity, calm and peace, and where the soul, in the presence of God's glorious and immaculate creation, is free from the chains of conventions, "forgets society and loosens its bonds with the strength of renewed youth; where every thought forms a prayer, where everything that is not in harmony with fresh, free nature disappears from the heart [and] ... the tired souls find rest, there the exhausted man regains his youthful strength" (*L,* 76). St. Francis too loosened his bond with society and journeyed to the wooded Mount La Verna, where "every thought [was] a prayer," and where "everything" was in "harmony [with] the heart." Van Gogh goes on to say to his brother that he should love a friend, a stranger, a wife, something—whatever it is—but that he should love "with a lofty and serious intimate sympathy, with strength, with intelligence; and ... must always try to know deeper, better and more. That leads to God" (*L*, 133). Thomas à Kempis, following in the footsteps of St. Francis and St. Augustine, writes that "love descends from God, and may not finally rest in anything lower than God."[20]

With à Kempis, St. Francis, and St. Augustine, van Gogh says the fruit of love is service, and applies it in writing to his brother, telling him that he should love the poor, the weavers, the farmers, the miners, the laborers, the people that walk the streets, the lowest of the low, for these are the people van Gogh wants to give voice, if only he could paint them (*L*, 136); these people know the very depths of misery; they have experienced suffering, pain, sorrow, sadness, hunger, destitution, homelessness; they live their lives in total darkness. Yet these people too, concludes van Gogh, "can have moments of emotion and inspiration which give him a feeling of an eternal home, and of being close to it" (*L*, 248), recalling a holy city referred to by St. Augustine as the city of God, and by Bunyan as a celestial city, illumined by the unchangeable light of God, the light that shines in the darkness which led St. John of the Cross on his journey to climb Mount Carmel where God was waiting for him, "In a place where no one else appeared";[21] that is, in the darkness of his soul, as in the miners, the workers, the homelessness, and van Gogh himself.

These are the people that St. Mother Teresa (1910-1997) also gives voice to in the slums of India; she too, like van Gogh, desires to give them "a feeling of an eternal home" which she also believes can be experienced through love, "the fire that will make them live the life to its full."[22] Similarly, St. Catherine of Siena also devoted her life to the poor, the sick, the victims of the black death; she too wanted to give these people "a feeling of an eternal home" based on love and, like St. Mother Teresa, St. Catherine also speaks of love as "the fire in [my] soul [which] grew so great that [my] body could not have contained it."[23] Before St. Catherine and St. Mother Teresa, St. Francis likewise had cared for the poor, for those afflicted with leprosy, for the beggars and, like van Gogh, he too experienced the bitterness of being rejected by his family, and of being called eccentric. In words comparable to those of these three mystics of the Church, van Gogh also defines love as "a great fire in our soul" whose flame lights up all that is hidden in our inner darkness, that burns so deeply within us, yet "no one ever comes to warm himself at it, and the passers-by see only a wisp of smoke coming through the chimney, and go along their way" (L, 133). Moreover, van Gogh, like these three Saints, considers love as that "*germinating force* ... in us" (L, W1), "that higher feeling which [one] cannot do without" (L, 159), for love perfects, transforms us, makes us reach to others, and, he concludes, "what is done in love is well done" (L, 121). As St. Augustine puts it, "No fruit is good which does not grow from the root of love,"[24] which, "like an ember or a spark of fire, flames always upward, by the fervor of its love, toward God," observes à Kempis.[25]

In contrast to the Catholic mystic who weds Christ and, therefore, the Church as bride, van Gogh yearns for a concrete realization of love; that is, for an intimate relationship with a woman. This brings van Gogh into a great conflict with the love preached by the clergymen of the Dutch Reformed Church, including his father who was a minister of that Church. To van Gogh, these clergymen preach a love that he finds impersonal, abstract, dogmatic, systematic, rational, and that triggers in him a crisis of faith: "'O God, there is no God!' For me that God of the clergymen is as dead as a doornail." He then asks his brother: "But am I an atheist for all that? The clergymen consider me so—so be it—but I love, and how could I feel love if I did not live and others did not live; and then if we live, there is something mysterious in that. Now call it God or human nature or whatever you like, but there is something which I cannot define systematically, though it is very much alive and very real" (L, 164). Hence what God is to the clergymen, to van Gogh is not real, not alive, not felt; it is "an empty sound" (L, 158); it is nonsense. One must "feel that there is a God, not dead or stuffed but alive" (L, 161) urging us toward loving, with pity, humility, sincerity, benevolence, patience, charity, and compassion—virtues that embody the very life of the Catholic mystic—but which van Gogh believes is not in the language of the clergymen. For this reason, he "reckon[s] the whole lot of them among the most ungodly men in our society" (L, 288). Van Gogh is of the opinion that the clergymen are too narrow-minded, too driven by bigotry, hypocrisy, and prejudices to understand the "modern soul" (L, 339a) in search of love, without which "I shall freeze or turn to stone" or live in "a sinful and immoral condition" (L, 164).

At their core, these words echo St. Francis; for, van Gogh, like St. Francis, calls on the Dutch Church to reform itself, to base its teachings on love which he, like St. Francis, believes is attained through "simplicity and truth" (L, 339a). Thomas à Kempis considers them the "two wings" that lift us from earthly things "toward God, and ... love samples and tastes"[26] the goodness of God's charity. We are pilgrims on this earth and strangers, says van Gogh to his brother, recalling *The Pilgrim's Progress*, *The Imitation of Christ*,[27] and St. Augustine's *The Confessions*. Our life might be compared to sailing on a river, van Gogh continues; "but very soon the waves become higher, the wind more violent, we are at sea almost before we are aware of it.... The heart of man is very much like the sea, it has its storms, its tides and its depths; it has its pearls too."[28] Like a sailor, van Gogh is being tossed to and from on a stormy sea, and asks, as does the sailor, whether he will ever reach port with "pearls" in his hands. Moreover, similar to the sailor who finds herself caught at sea in the midst of violent wind and high waves, as though incapable of freeing herself, van Gogh likewise sees himself "a prisoner," "a caged bird ... maddened by anguish" for being unable to free himself from "certain barriers, certain gates, certain walls," asking: "My God! is it for long, is it forever, is it for all eternity?" (L, 133) As with the sailor, who knows that the sea is dangerous and the storm terrible, yet lets his love for the sea compel him not to remain ashore in spite of these dangers, so with van Gogh, whose love of and for art compel him to seek, to strive, to hopefully reach port, notwithstanding the risk of losing his life. Van Gogh tells his brother that this love is also the love that called Socrates who, "by devotion, work and renouncing frivolous things," imbued his life with "a ray of light from heaven" (L, 306). The life of the Catholic mystic is similarly a life of "devotion, work and renouncing frivolous things," as well as a life with "its storms, its tides and its depths; it has its pearls too"—as, for example, *The Imitation of Christ*, *The Confessions* of St. Augustine, the *Dialogue* of St. Catherine of Siena, *The Ascent of Mount Carmel* of St. John of the Cross, and *Come be My Light* of St. Mother Teresa.

Van Gogh confesses to his brother that life is not as simple or cut and dried for the "modern soul" as clergymen make it appear; for, if it were so it wouldn't be very difficult to make one's way. But it isn't, and things are infinitely more complicated, and right and wrong do not exist separately, any more than black and white do in nature; there are things that remain incomprehensible and dark before "the cold light of reason and calculation" (L, 259). Besides, van Gogh insists, the clergymen do not know that religious life other than their own exist; they do not know that God's love extends towards evil and the unrighteous as well. As to those who sincerely, honestly, patiently, and humbly seek their own path with sympathy and deep love, van Gogh reminds his brother that, as Victor Hugo writes, "*Il y a le rayon noir et il y a le rayon blanc* [There is a black ray and there is a white ray]" (L, 326). The clergymen, concludes van Gogh, have "a black ray," which he associates with hypocrisy; whereas he seeks the "White Light" (L, 339a), which is simplicity and truth. He says that, where simplicity does not exist, truth turns into lies, into hypocrisy, which affects a false piety, vanity (L, 345a). The soul of a Thomas à Kempis serves van Gogh as a mirror of the simplicity and truth of Christ reflecting the simplicity and truth of God (L, 116).

Van Gogh's search for the "White Light" or for "a ray from on high" (L, 242) leads him on the path to his love of art as analogous to his love for a woman; and van Gogh's love for Christine Clasina Maria Hoornik, known as Sien—a prostitute of thirty years of age, sick and alcoholic, and who became his companion, his mistress, and his model—teaches van Gogh the cold and false love that the clergymen preach; for Christ, unlike what the clergymen preach, allowed a prostitute to kiss his feet (*Luke* 7: 37-39), and spoke words of hope to outcast women (*John* 4: 7-27; 8:11). It is this loving attitude of Christ that van Gogh sees in the books he read, and in the works of art he saw as he wandered from place to place arousing in him a "violent passion for them, reaching the highest pitch of enthusiasm" (L, 133). Now, if Christ is "a greater artist than all other artists" (L, B8[11]), and if Christ is God's love made flesh, then, the end of love and of art is an end itself. Hence van Gogh writes to his traveling companion and artist Anton van Rappard: "Let us give our souls to our cause, let us work with our heart, and truly love what we love.... One loves because one loves. To love ... that is all!" (L, R5, 156)

These words circle us to St. Bernard of Clairvaux (1090-1153) who, borrowing from Augustine's *De Doctrine Christiana* I.1, writes: "I love because I love [*Amo quia amo*]; I love that I may love. Love is a great thing; as long as it returns to its beginning, goes back to its origin, turns again to its source, it will always draw afresh from it and flow freely.... Love needs no cause, no fruit besides itself; its enjoyment is its use."[29] Like St.

Bernard, van Gogh says that love is something infinite, deep, eternal (*L*, 276), and that it demands self-sacrifice or the loss of the self; and, like St. Bernard, van Gogh believes that in physical love there is truly the presence of God, that fountain of fire that "wells up from a deeper source in our souls" (*L*, R43) so as to inflame our thirsty soul so as to yearn for its Eternal Spring whose clarity, says St. John of the Cross, "is never darkened, / And I know that every light has / come from it / Although it is night." Therefore, love, like art, demands that the self "be dead to everything" (*L*, 313); and art, like love, is something greater and higher than technical skill; it is a "mystery," a "blessing" (*L* 266), "a ray of light from heaven." It is, in sum, "the fire in our soul" which is the Creator Spirit: "*Veni, Creator Spiritus* ... and in our souls take up Thy rest ... to Thee we cry, o heavenly gift of God Most High ... o fount of life and fire of love."[30]

As "heavenly gift" or as "fount of life" or as "fire of love," the Creator Spirit is love as spiritual seeing;[31] it is the enlightened eye, the eye of "inner silence" (*L*, 333) that penetrates to the invisible, to depths of things, to the light that renders everything beautiful; for, says van Gogh, there is nothing more truly creative than to remain silent—which Jacques Maritain (1882-1973) calls "internal fruition"[32]—as one looks with awe at the wonders of creation. As often as van Gogh finds himself among the company of artists, he always finds it difficult to speak about "simple [things] in themselves, but which are unfortunately connected with much deeper things" (*L*, 313)—which, in my opinion, will undo him, since he has no one with whom to share the silence of these "deeper things."[33] Hence "How can I express myself? I want to be silent" (*L*, R4) about the love for "deeper things," a love that demands nothing more than total self-surrender.

"Surrender is also true love," observes Mother Teresa. "The more we surrender, the more we love God and souls.... Total surrender—for us, contemplative life means also a joyous and ardent response to his call to the most intimate union with him."[34] As in the contemplative, so in van Gogh, without this total self-surrender, the heart *loves* nature, but this love is rational, and abstract. Even if one loves nature, van Gogh goes on to say, she remains distant and absent. Though nature's intentions are "beauty and sublimity," yet she leaves one "cold and without emotion." In art, van Gogh writes to Rappard, "beauty and sublimity" are sought in an intimate contact with nature otherwise the result is "false"; it is an art that freezes, petrifies, and prevents "a warmer, a more fruitful love from awakening in you." Hence van Gogh urges Rappard to let go of his academic "mistress, and fall desperately in love with Dame Nature or Reality" (L, R4), as van Gogh himself does. Van Gogh's love for Lady Nature or Reality mirrors his love for Sien, "a pregnant woman who had to walk the streets" (L, 192), and whom the clergymen view as a sinner. But van Gogh believes that in his love for Sien, he lives out the vey mystery of God's love (L, W1), as he does in his love for Lady Nature.

Unlike Rappard's cold and barren "mistress," van Gogh's Lady Nature warms, refreshes, gives life, and is "a *woman* born of a woman." She knows "how to love and craves for love," for she possesses sincerity of feelings; she dwells not in Heaven but on earth. She is "goodness, kindness, tenderness"; she is true "beauty and sublimity" (L, R4). In simplicity, poverty, solitude, silence and quiet (L, 133, 253, 543)—ideas that take us back not only to Francis of Assisi but also to the Catholic mystical tradition in general—one learns to love her, and that a joyful encounter with her also embraces sorrow and pain, for "the more one has intercourse with [her]" (L, R43), the more painful it is to unveil the secret of her heart; for, "I cannot say that I have won her by a long shot, but what I *can* say is that ... I am trying to find the key to her heart," notwithstanding at times the pain, the "exhaustion and impatience" (L, R4). True art is achieved only through an "intercourse" with Nature—as love is through an intimate communion or "intercourse" with a woman, concludes van Gogh: "I cannot live without love, without a woman. I would not value life at all, if there were not something infinite, something deep, something real" (L, 164).

These words take us back to Genesis 2, when God created Adam, saying: "It is not good for man to be alone" (*Gen* 2: 18). After creating the animals, God created Eve from Adam's ribs. "This at last," he exclaims, "this one is bone of my bones and flesh of my flesh" (*Gen* 2: 23). Thus in awakening, Adam not only discovers that he is missing part of himself but he also discovers Eve as complementing him. So only in union with Eve will Adam recover his complete self, or what he has lost. Thus in sexual love or "intercourse," Adam and Eve complete each other, and that without the other each is missing "something infinite, something deep, something real." St. John of the Cross gives the mystical treatment of this union of love: "Love produces such likeness in this transformation of lovers that one can say each is the other and both are one. The reason is, that in the union and transformation of love each gives possession of self to the other, and each leaves and exchanges self for the other. Thus each one lives in the other and is the other, and both are one in the transformation of love."[35]

That van Gogh cannot "live without love, without a woman," is not only an analogue for his spiritual truth but also for his art as an "intercourse" with Lady Nature; and Lady Nature who personifies Sien—"a *woman* born of a woman"—as model for art and for love itself, a love that inspires van Gogh to create (L R34). Hence in an art created with love (L 309), van Gogh glimpses the "White Light," or the "ray from on high," not on the basis of the "cold academic view" (L, 164, 133), but on the *fire of love* as the "modern soul" journeys into God's ineffable graciousness in Christ who, says van Gogh, uses images from art to convey his meaning: "[His] spoken words ... are one of the highest summits—the very highest summit—reached by art, which becomes a creative force.... They make us see the art of creating life, the art of being immortal and alive at the same time. They are connected with painting" (L, B8 [11]) as mirror of the mystery of Love, of Light, of Eternity, "which the halo used to symbolize, and which we seek to convey by the actual radiance and vibration of our coloring" (L, 531).

By emphasizing "the halo," Van Gogh takes us back to a world far different from ours, to a world, he says, painted by "Dante, Petrarch, Boccaccio, Giotto and Botticelli" with the "fullness of goodness and ardor"—though he prefers the artist rather than the poet, because "the artist ... is silent" (L, 539). So too the mystic is "silent." And for the mystic God is Silence, is a friend of silence. "Nature: trees, flowers, and grass grow in silence," writes St. Mother Teresa, and "The stars, the moon and the sun move in silence.... We need silence to be able to touch souls ... to find God" [36] in Christ's fleshly love or *erös* on the Cross. As Hans Urs von Balthasar observes:

> In the face of the Cross, love is sobered to its very marrow before God's *agape*, which clothes itself in the language of the body; and, in the face of this intoxicating language of flesh and blood that gives itself by being poured out, love is lifted above itself and

elevated into the eternal, in order there, as creaturely *eros,* to be the tent and dwelling-place of the divine love! Love is dispossessed in order to become the expression of something higher.[37]

Sensuous images of divine radiance and love

Van Gogh sees nature filled with the *fire* of God's divine love as light, and through the vibrations of colors he imparts on things an inner luminosity and a radiance that renders them a "living Presence"—real, true, vivid, animated, yet partaking of the infinite, of the eternal, of the mystery, as do the things or figures that Michelangelo and Millet depict (*L,* 418). Paradoxically, Michelangelo and Millet paint like Evangelical Protestants,[38] yet they are Catholics; conversely, van Gogh, whose upbringing was Protestant, but who later embraced Evangelism, paints like a Catholic. Above and beyond this, Michelangelo and Millet are seen by van Gogh as mirroring similar religious struggles that he experiences in their art; their art, van Gogh observes, does not depict "things as they are, traced in a dry analytical way, but as *they* ... feel them"; that is, with "those very incorrectnesses, those deviations, remodelings, changes in reality, so that they become, yes, lies if you like—but truer than the literal truth" (*L,* 418). What van Gogh wants us to experience as we contemplate his works are feelings of sincerity, of warmth, of intimacy, of serenity, of calm, and of purity. It is true that we often encounter van Gogh in a state of anger, anxiety, passion, and changing moods; yet deep within his heart there always remains "a calm pure harmony and music inside me" (*L,* 218). Equally true is that van Gogh's life is filled with suffering, sorrow, failures, and disappointments—as are the lives of Michelangelo and Millet—yet his art reflects the radiance of love: the "White light," the "ray of light from heaven," "grace" (*L,* 238), which is Love and Life in their inexhaustible mystery, in their the inaccessible Light, in their deep Silence.

Van Gogh's paintings of the simple lives of the farmers—the farmers that till the earth, that load a boat, that plant potatoes, that dig potatoes, that eat potatoes, that rest at noon and watch a little girl take her first steps at the end of the day, as well as his paintings of the solitary farmer sowing, cultivating, and harvesting—all reveal the forms under which this mystery of love, this inaccessible light, and this deep silence is experienced, paralleling the daily solitary work of the contemplative who, in the words of Dom R. Sorg, "gravitates towards art. For in God's service [the monk] must never be less than an artist.... All work ... is art when its mind is Godward."[39] Van Gogh's works are mindful of God, and as such they *participate* in divine love as ordinary as eating potatoes, as sowing, as digging, as resting, as sunrise and sunset, as streaming water, and as fields of grain and of olives. Like van Gogh's farmer, the contemplative also lives in close contact "with the earth, sky, and sea ... the bright running stream, the easy gifts which mother earth ...yields on very little persuasion."[40] For the contemplative, as for van Gogh's farmer, all created things manifest God's glorious work of creation and refer to him by way of prayerful reading and physical labor (*ora et labora*). St. Benedict (c. 480-547) writes: "Let us open our eyes to the light that comes from God, and our ears to the voice from heaven that every day calls us" to do our daily work with love as/and obedience.[41]

Van Gogh's life and works somewhat echo St. Benedict's call. In fact, the artist writes to his brother Theo, saying: "*Ora* et labora, let us do our daily work ... with all our strength and let us believe that God will give good gifts" (*L*, 39). His work, the *Potatoes Eaters at a Table* (1885), for example, emphasizes "that those people, eating their potatoes in the lamplight, have dug the earth with those very hands they put in the dish, and so it speaks of *manual labor*" (*L*, 404). Consequently, it alludes to St. Benedict who in *Rule* 35 says that the monks should serve one another and God in the meal, and that the utensils and the goods they use should be washed. Hence St. Benedict regards them as sacred, for they reveal God's love for us in Christ on the Cross—"the Great Man of Sorrows" (*L*, 127).

Hence the *Potatoes Eaters at a Table* is analogous to the sacrament of the Holy Communion or Eucharist. The figures are shown in the acts of giving, of sharing, of thoughtfulness, of thankfulness, of attentiveness, of kindness, of tenderness, of serenity, of empathy, of reverence, of peace and of muted joy, as though the oil lamp suspended from the ceiling spreads light inside the dark house as the Eucharist does in the hearts or souls of the figures transporting them on the wings of "simplicity and truth" beyond the confines of their earthly and dark existence. "You [Theo] know how one of the roots or foundations, not only of the Gospel, but of the whole Bible is 'Light that rises in the darkness'" (*L*, 126); that essential paradox that constitutes the very mystic way. Not only does light shine in the darkness of these farmers eating at a table, but it also lights their poses, gestures, and expressions thus speaking the unspeakable. Everything in this work is quiet, motionless, waiting, yet everything speaks, is in motion, is present or sacramental: "The table is their altar and the food a sacrament for which each has labored," observes Meyer Shapiro.[42]

Just as van Gogh associates "the food" with the dark existence of the poor and with "the Great Man of Sorrows," the contemplative too regards the Eucharist as inseparable from Christ on the Cross and from the darkness of the poor. Mother Teresa writes: "In the Eucharist, I see Christ [on the Cross] in the appearance of bread. In the slums, I see Christ in the distressing disguise of the poor."[43] Moreover, the contemplative, like van Gogh, glimpses God's light in the darkness, a darkness so dark that Mother Teresa, like van Gogh, cries out: "I am alone.—Unwanted, forsaken.—The loneliness of the heart that wants love is unbearable."[44] She calls on the Sisters of the Missionaries of Charity, as van Gogh calls on the ministers of the Dutch Reformed Church, to go forth into the world and work with great patience, love and care so as to keep the light of God burning. She tells the Sisters that the way of becoming God's light is by being sincere, kind, loving, thoughtful, truthful, and humble towards others; for, it is in their being humble that love becomes real, devoted, and a living flame consuming the selfishness that prevents spiritual and creative growth. "[To] keep your lamp burning," says Mother Teresa to the Sisters, you have to keep putting "drops of oil in [it]. What are these drops of oil in our lamps? They are the small things of daily life."[45] This metaphor of the oil lamp takes us back to van Gogh's *Potatoes Eaters at a Table* where to do God's simple work is love, which keeps the "lamp burning." Van Gogh writes: "One must keep something of the original character of a Robinson Crusoe or an anchorite, for otherwise one has no root in oneself, and one must never let the fire in one's soul die, but keep it burning" (L, 121).

"Flood my soul with your spirit and life / Penetrate and possess my whole being so utterly / that all my life may only be a radiance of yours, / Shine through me.... / So to shine as to be a light to others."[46] These words come from Mother Teresa's favorite prayer which she borrows from Cardinal John Henry Newman; but they could easily have come from van Gogh as well who in *The Reaper* (1889) and *Noon: Rest from Work* (1890) depicts the life of the "spirit," not in the light of the sun, but through the simultaneity and contrasts of colors, such as yellow, blue, gray, purple, and green; the silent melody of love's *work and rest* swells forth as to suggest the rhythmic day of the contemplative life in harmony with nature's cycles. In these works, the "spirit" does shine brightly on the lives of these ordinary, humble, and working farmers as they do "small things of daily life"; but it also shines through van Gogh whose eyes of silence perceive God's everlasting or eternal Light (*L* 82a, 112), which the color rhythms or vibrations intend to express. "Revelation of spirit by means of colour: that was Van Gogh's dream," writes Lionello Venturi.[47]

It is color, then, that opens the world of the reapers and of the farmers at rest to illumination, as if seen from an unseen light that, in my opinion, recalls the works of Simone Martini (1284-1344) and Fra Angelico (1400-1455), where the rhythmic use of color, especially yellow, sets everything aflame with the fire of divine love as light "unknown to the eye and yet … pleasing to the sight";[48] and, as in van Gogh, so in Simone Martini and Fra Angelico, the figures are imbued with life, yet they are contemplative, empathic, reverential, at rest, as it were. However, in contrast to van Gogh, where light is real, in Fra Angelico and Simone Martini, light is ideal, and the space is only partially depicted, not through shadow or *chiaroscuro*, as in van Gogh, but by soft and delicate lines. Nonetheless, *The Reaper, Noon: Rest from Work*, and the works of Simone Martini and Fra Angelico, speak of painting as divine light, and of divine light as painting aesthetically or poetically beautiful to suggest another world, not of earth but of heaven, not of the finite but of the infinite, not of saying but of the unsaying, not of the temporal but of the eternal, "which the halo used to symbolize." In van Gogh's works, as in the works of Simone Martini and Fra Angelico, we have a "symphony of yellow" (*L*, 429),[49] or a poetry of light that is heavenly beautiful painted by hands with the *fire of love* within "the dark night of the soul," which for St. John of the Cross is the light of faith, as it is also for van Gogh who, like St. John, journeys alone and in darkness along the mystical way of the "holy longing" of love.

Just as St. John of the Cross sees everything in nature as alluding to God's light, which his poetry praises, so does van Gogh. Van Gogh, like St. John, sees nature not as the whole of reality, nor as God; rather, as manifesting God who remains hidden from us. Nature is in God, and God is in nature: they are distinct, yet connected or united, as are religion and art, writes van Gogh to Theo (*L,* 49). Like St. John, van Gogh looks on nature as a field of symbols or metaphors that lead him to God, but only if our relation with nature is a love union based on simplicity, truth, sincerity, gratitude, reverence, and humility, a union where nature and the self are distinct, and not where the self merges with nature, as in romanticism or pantheism.[50] When van Gogh confesses to his brother Theo that he has "a terrible need of--shall I say the word?--religion. Then I go out ... to paint the stars" (*L,* 543)—the sun, the moon, the clouds, the rain, the wind, the birds or crows, butterflies, trees, cypresses, poplars, blooming chestnut branches, olive trees, sunflowers, field with poppies, irises, blades of grass, running water, mountains and valleys, wood and stones, churches and houses—he is saying that through his artistic creativity he appears more and more in the image of God in Christ as "great artist" (*L,* B8[11]), and is led by everything in nature to contemplate the supreme Craftsman, the *Creator Spiritus,* and to offer him hymns of praises in the forms of sensuous images or symbols.

Hence these works may be seen as psalms or poems or songs without words; indeed, they may be seen as images for contemplation, for meditation, for prayer; they may serve as our silent dialogue before the hidden God leading us from darkness to light, as for example *Saying Grace* (1883), and *Woman Praying* (1883). At a time when we no longer believe in God or when God's light is no longer perceived by us, and when we no longer consider love as "sacred territory," art can provide an image of our divine existence. Such art is visible in Vincent van Gogh; it is visible because, in the words of Etienne Gilson (1884-1978),

> to be creative is to imitate, in a finite and analogical way, the divine prerogative, exclusively reserved for He Who Is, of making things to be. Now ... to make things to be and to make them beautiful are one and the same things. Each artist, then, while exerting his often anguished effort to add new types of beings to those which make up the world of nature, should be conscious of the resemblance between his finite art and the infinitely perfect efficacy of the divine power. All truly creative art is religious in its own right.[51]

The art of van Gogh "is religious in its own right," yet it may be seen as an analogue of Catholic mysticism; not in every aspect, to be sure. Like the Catholic mystics, van Gogh resorts to the beautiful metaphor of the *spark* or *fire* or *flame* to express his *holy yearning* for love and light that he seeks. Moreover, as with St. Teresa of Avila, who likens the mystical life of contemplation or prayer to a "silkworm" transforming into a "white butterfly,"[52] so too van Gogh compares the artist's existence to "the caterpillar" transforming "into a butterfly" (*L*, B8 [11]). Both lives reflecting one another are veiled in darkness, are bathed in tears of the *fire* of love, yet both testify to the unchangeable or inaccessible light of God, and to joy; both lives are rooted in humility, poverty, self-denial, simplicity, honesty, truth, sincerity, reverence, solitude, and silence; and both lives bear witness to the "modern soul" traveling toward the Heavenly City where God will turn their lives completely into *fire* by the light of his love: the song of joy, "the very music of the heart," tells us St. Bernard. "It is not a sound from the lips but a stirring of joy, not a harmony of voices but of wills," St. Bernard continues. "It is not heard outwardly, nor does it sound in public.... Only he who sings it hears it, and he to whom it is sung—the Bride and the Bridegroom. It is a wedding song indeed, expressing ... the concord of their lives and the mutual exchange of their love."[53]

Notes

1. May, Simon, *Love: A History* (New Haven, CT: Yale University Press, 2011), p. xi.
2. Teresa of Avila, *The Way of Perfection*, trans., ed. E. Allison Peers (Garden City, NY: Image Books, 1964), chap. 6, p. 27.
3. Augustine, *The Confessions of St. Augustine*, trans. Rex Warner (New York: New American Library, 1963), bk. X, p. 27.
4. James, William, *The Varieties of Religious Experiences* (New York: The Modern Library, 1994), p. 435.
5. John of the Cross, "The Spiritual Canticle," in *The Collected Works of St. John of the Cross*, trans. Kieran Kavanaugh, O.C., and Otilio Rodriguez, O.C.D. (Garden City, NY: Double Day & Company, Inc., 1964).
6. Berdyaev, Nicolas, *The Destiny of Man*, trans, Natalie Duddington, M. A. (London: Geoffrey Bles, 1954), pp. 147-48.
7. See Edwards, Cliff, *Van Gogh and God: A Creative Spiritual Quest* (Chicago, IL: Loyola University Press, 1989); and Erickson, Kathleen P., *At Eternity's Gate: The Spiritual Vision of Vincent Van Gogh* (Grand Rapids, MI: Eerdmans, 1998).
8. Silverman, Debora, *Van Gogh and Gauguin: The Search for Sacred Art* (New York: Farrar, Strauss and Giroux, 2000).
9. Augustine, *The Confessions of St. Augustine*, trans. Rex Warner., bk. VII, 10.

10. van Gogh, Vincent, *The Complete Letters of Vincent van Gogh*, 2nd ed., 3 vols. (Boston, MA: A Bulfinch Press Book, 1978), Letter 126. Hereafter abbreviated in the text as *L*.
11. Catherine of Siena, *Catherine of Siena: The Dialogue*, trans. Suzanne Noffke, O. P. (New York: Paulist Press, 1980), chap. 1, 25.
12. Nicholas of Cusa, "On the Vision of God," in *Nicholas of Cusa: Selected Spiritual Writings*, trans. H. Lawrence Bond (New York and Mahwah: Paulist Press, 1997), preface, 235.
13. Sweetman, David, *Van Gogh: His Life and His Art* (New York: Crown Publishers, Inc., 1990), p. 149.
14. John of the Cross, "Song of the Soul that Rejoices in Knowing God through Faith," in *The Collected Works of St. John of the Cross*, trans. Kieran Kavanaugh, O.C., and Otilio Rodriguez, O.C.D., prologue, and stanza 5.
15. Catherine of Siena, *Catherine of Siena: The Dialogue*, trans. Suzanne Noffke, O. P., chap. 92, 170.
16. Weil, Simone, *Gravity and Grace*, trans. Emma Craufurd (London: Routledge & Kegan Paul, 1952), p. 137.
17. Francis of Assisi, "The Canticle of Brother Sun," in *Bonaventure: The Soul's Journey into God; The Tree of Life; The Life of St. Francis*, trans. Ewert Cousins (New York: Paulist Press, 1978), p. 28. See also von Balthasar, Hans Urs, *Seeing the Form*, 33, where he claims that splendor and form produce in us a transport of love which belongs to the very origin of Christianity: "The Apostles were transported by what they saw, heard, and touched—by everything manifested in the form."
18. See Sund, Judy, *True Temperament: Van Gogh and French Naturalist Literature* (Cambridge: Cambridge University Press, 1992).
19. See van Uitert, Evert, "Vincent van Gogh: A Literary Life," http://www.vggallery.com/index.html.
20. Thomas à Kempis, *The Imitation of Christ*, trans. S. J., ed. Harold C. Gardiner Richard Whitford (New York: Image Books, 1955), bk. III, 5.
21. John of the Cross, "The Dark Night," in *The Collected Works of St. John of the Cross*, trans. Kieran Kavanaugh, O.C., and Otilio Rodriguez, O.C.D., prologue, and pp. 295-96.
22. Mother Teresa, *Mother Teresa: Come be My Light: The Private Writings of the "Saint of Calcutta,"* ed. Brian Kolodiejchuk, M. C. (New York: Doubleday, 2007), p. 50.
23. Catherine of Siena, *Catherine of Siena: The Dialogue*, trans. Suzanne Noffke, O. P., 13, 48.
    Catherine of Siena, *Catherine of Siena: The Dialogue*, trans. Suzanne Noffke, O. P., 13, 48.
24. Augustine, "On the Spirit and the Letter," in *Basic Writings of St. Augustine*, trans. P. Holmes (New York: Random House, 1948), bk. XXVI, 482.
25. Thomas à Kempis, *The Imitation of Christ*, trans. S. J., ed. Harold C. Gardiner Richard Whitford, bk. III, 5.
26. Ibid., bk. II, 4.
27. Ibid., bk. I, 23.
28. Van Gogh, "Vincent's Sermon," in *The Complete Letters of Vincent van Gogh*, vol. 1, 88.
29. Bernard of Clairvaux, *Bernard of Clairvaux: Selected Works*, trans. G. R. Evans (New York/Mahwah: Paulist Press, 1987), Sermon 83.4.
30. *Hymn of Vespers on Pentecost*, http://chantblog.blogspot.com/2008/05/hymns-for-pentecost.html.

31. See Kessler, Herbert L., *Spiritual Seeing: Picturing God's Invisibility in Medieval Art* (Philadelphia: University of Pennsylvania Press, 2000).
32. This accords with Maritain's concept of "connaturality" as a mysticism of self-expression, as an "internal fruition" born in the pre-conscious life of the intellect, and it is essentially an obscure revelation, a flash of reality out of sleep in one single awakening. See Maritan, *Creative Intuition*, pp. 11-134; Maritain, *The Range of Reason* (New York: Charles Scribner's Sons, 1952). See also John G- Jr. Trapani, *Poetry, Beauty and Contemplation: The Complete Aesthetics of Jacques Maritain* (Washington D.C.: Catholic University of America Press, 2011).
33. See Venturi, Lionello, *Impressionists and Symbolists*, trans. Francis Steegmuller (New York: Cooper Square Publishers, Inc., 1973), vol. 2, p. 188.
34. Mother Teresa, *Mother Teresa Essential Writings*, ed. Jean Maalouf (Maryknoll, NY: Orbis Books, 2001), p. 40.
35. John of the Cross, "The Spiritual Canticle," in *The Collected Works of St. John of the Cross*, trans. Kieran Kavanaugh, O.C., and Otilio Rodriguez, O.C.D., stanza 12, 7.
36. Mother Teresa, *No Greater Love*, ed. Becky Benenate & Joseph Durepos (Novato, CA: New World Library, 1997), pp. 8-10.
37. von Balthasar, Hans Urs, *Seeing the Form*, trans. Erasmo Leiva-Merikakis, ed. Joseph Fessio and John Riches (San Francisco: Ignatius Press, 1982), vol. 1, p. 673.
38. Michelangelo belonged to a group of Italian Evangelicals known as the *spirituali* who stressed the concept of *sola fide* and, therefore, of personal relationship to God in Christ. See in particular Jung, Eva Maria, 1953, "On the Nature of Evangelismo in Sixteenth-Century Italy," *Journal of the History of Ideas* 14, pp. 511-27; Nagel, Alexander, 1997, "Gifts for Michelangelo and Vittoria Colonna," *Art Bulletin* 79, pp. 647-55; and Caponetto, Salvatore, *The Protestant Reformation in Sixteenth-Century Italy*, trans. Anne C. Tedeschi and John Tedeschi (Kirksville, MO: Thomas Jefferson University Press, 1999).
39. Dom, R. Sorg, *Towards a Benedictine Theology of Manual Labor* (Lisle, IL: St. Procopius Abbey, 1951), p. 118.
40. Cardinal Newman, John Henry, "Benedictine Schools," in *Essays and Sketches*, 3 vols. (New-York : Longmans, Green and Co., 1948), vol. 3, p. 245.
41.. Benedict, *The Rule of St. Benedict*, ed. T. Fry (Collegeville, MN: Liturgical Press, 1981), prologue.
42. Schapiro, Meyer, *Vincent van Gogh* (New York: Harry N. Abrams, 1950), p. 50.
43. Mother Teresa, "A Joyful Life," in *Mother Teresa: Essential Writings*, ed. Jean Maalouf, pp. 100-1.
44. Mother Teresa, *Mother Teresa: Come be My Light: The Private Writings of the "Saint of Calcutta,"* ed. Brian Kolodiejchuk, M. C., p. 187.
45. Mother Teresa, *No Greater Love*, ed. Becky Benenate & Joseph Durepos, p. 22.
46. Ibid., p. 158.
47. Venturi, Lionello, *Impressionists and Symbolists*, trans. Francis Steegmuller (New York, NY: Cooper Square Publishers, Inc., 1973), p. 186.
48. Nicholas of Cusa, "On Seeking God," in *Nicholas of Cusa: Selected Spiritual Writings*, trans. H. Lawrence Bond, II, p. 35.

49. The theme of music in van Gogh is explored by Veldhorst, Natascha, *Van Gogh and Music: A Symphony in Blue and Yellow,* trans. Diane Webb (New Haven, CT: Yale University Press, 2018).
50. See Murray, Ann H., 1978, "The Religious Background of Vincent van Gogh and Its Relation to His Views on Nature and Art," *Journal of the American Academy of Religion,* 46, Supplement, pp. 67-96.
51. Gilson, Étienne, *Painting and Reality* (New York: Pantheon Books, 1957), p. 294.
52. Teresa of Avila, "Fifth Mansions," in *Interior Castle,* trans., ed. E. Allison Peers (Garden City, NY: Image Books, 1961), chap. 2.
53. Bernard of Clairvaux, *Bernard of Clairvaux: Selected Works,* trans. G. R. Evans, Sermon 1.

CROSSCURRENTS

LET US NEVER FORGET

Bob Blundell

In a secluded forest near the city of Krakow, a young sentry stood watch. Muted rays of sunlight filtered through the pines casting a pale light on the soldier, just a boy of 17. A tattered grey uniform sagged over his thin frame and the silver eagle on his helmet was faded to the color of dust. The emblem, denoting him as an infantryman in the army of the Third Reich, had once been a symbol of pride and honor. But those days had long since passed.

Though it was early Spring, a biting wind whispered softly through the treetops, and he raised his collar and peered up into a morning sky turned murky grey. He felt the moist sting of snowflakes on his cheeks and closed his eyes, reflecting on more tranquil times. His mind began to drift and for a moment he could see his loving mother's face, the noble lines of age etched above her lips, and the gentle creases beneath deep azure eyes. But soon the image faded, and he returned to this place and time. He wiped a smudge from his watch and stared pensively back toward the camp below him, watching the soldiers scurry about in preparation.

Soon the trains would come, and the madness would begin.

A tall SS colonel, hardened by years of combat in north Africa, strutted from the comforting warmth of his barracks and quietly surveyed the expanse of rail tracks stretching to the south. He lit a cigarette with his right hand and exhaled, sending a blue plume of smoke drifting into the frigid air. His left arm dangled uselessly at his side and a serpentine scar snaked along the length of his jaw.

Both were remnants of his service to the cause. He had been selected for this commission because he had spent his life devoted to the fatherland. But more important, there was a harsh coldness in his heart that suited this task well.

Thin strands of ice clung to the barbed wire stretching around the camp, and he seemed to regard this curiously. He stood in the early morning mist, pacing and smoking his cigarette, then tossed it to the ground and began to shout orders to the troops.

The young soldier and his comrades moved to their assigned positions, and within minutes the ground began to rumble, and the mechanical grind of the locomotive pierced the air as it lumbered toward the camp. Suddenly the face of the engine broke through a silver fog hovering over the tracks, and it crept toward them slowly like a great beast. It's bones creaked as its weight was absorbed by the steel rails, and when it finally came to a stop, it uttered a loud sigh like a mournful mother.

The soldiers quickly began their business of unloading the cargo as terrified screams filtered through the tired wooden slats of the cars. The victims, men, women, and children poured through the narrow doors and some stumbled to the icy ground to be trampled by those behind them.

The officer watched this melee with no emotion, then strutted to the entrance of the camp and waited while the people were herded into two lines. As the innocents marched past him, he studied them carefully as a farmer would view livestock for purchase. The strongest would be chosen for a slow death through starvation, and disease. The rest would be ushered into the buildings for disposal.

The first group of women and children were herded into the courtyard by guards brandishing rifles with bayonets. The wet steel of the blades glistened like teeth in the morning mist, and the terrified shrieks of frightened children filled the air. After they had been carefully counted, they were ordered to remove their clothing. They slowly disrobed, dropping their garments to the snow, and as their bodies were exposed, the soldiers laughed, shouting taunts and jeers. The women huddled against one another, covering their breasts, and shivered under an icy mist that fell like tears from the sky.

Towels and bars of soap were distributed to some, and they were told they would be cleansed in the showers before entry into their barracks. These words of deception calmed many of them as they made their way into the red brick structure.

When the building was filled, the heavy oak doors were closed and locked behind them. Minutes later, the canisters would be opened, and cyanide gas would pour from the vents in the ceiling. Seeing the pale blue vapors descend upon them, they would shriek in horror and frantically scratch and claw at the doors imprisoning them. Some would die within minutes, but others lasted longer.

When the chamber had been safely ventilated and the bodies removed, the process would begin again.

The young sentry stood silently at his post, feeling the warmth of tears on his cheeks, knowing what he would he had seen and been a part of, would haunt him the rest of his days.

I am in southern Poland, at a place known as Auschwitz. It's a word that brings an aura of darkness and gloom to those who hear it. Over a million innocent people were systematically exterminated here as part of the Nazi's final solution.

Remnants of the horror still stand, a reminder of the evil that can exist in men's hearts. Rusty tracks bearing the trains filled with victims, are still intact. Wooden buildings housing prisoners under unspeakable conditions, stand alongside the gas chambers and incinerators, horrific reminders of the atrocities that existed here.

I walk through a dimly lit hallway in a building that has witnessed grief and sorrow beyond what most of us can imagine. Its walls are lined with photos of those who suffered and died here. Their eyes stare at me, dark and vacuous, pleading, crying out for mercy. A mercy that never came.

Cobbled streets meander through the camp. The stones are ash in color and splintered and cracked from age. The tears and blood spilled on these pathways have long since washed away, but I can sense sorrow and despair once flowed here like a raging river. I close my eyes and smell the stench of the bodies being incinerated and hear the panicked cries of pain drifting over me like a macabre mist lingering over the forest.

Twisted strings of barbed wire still encircle the encampment. I see the gaunt, broken bodies of those who may have chosen a quicker death by attempting escape. Their emaciated corpses hang suspended in the air, entwined in the harsh teeth of the metal strands, ravaged by the bullets from the machine guns guarding the camp.

The gallows, where thousands were publicly executed, stand tall and forthright in the courtyard. I see the victims' bodies twist slowly in the breeze. The ropes around their necks creak as they tighten under the victims' weight. Their feet flail about in desperation and the cords cut deeply into their flesh, until they gasp their last frantic breath. A gruesome message of obedience or death, to those who lived there.

The ones who were chosen by the Germans to remain at Auschwitz faced an incarceration filled with hardship and suffering. Prisoners were relegated to harsh conditions with barracks barren of heat, toilets, or other basic comforts required in civilized society. Many died of starvation or from lack of hope for a better existence.

My steps take me into the last building. On display are thousands of tiny shoes and boots from the children who were savagely exterminated, a horrific message even the young and innocent are not immune to the evil in the world. Tears fill my eyes and I marvel how any human being could inflict such suffering on another.

I could never have imagined a place so somber, so absent of light. Despair surrounds Auschwitz like a dark fog, stifling one's ability to put into words what is seen and felt here. As a member of the same human race guilty of committing these atrocities, I am ashamed and horrified such evil could have existed in modern society.

Some may ask, *'How could God allow this to happen?'*

I consider this question, as I envision the faces of the millions who must have stared into the heavens crying out for deliverance from their torment.

But it wasn't God who perpetrated this misery. It was the wickedness in men's hearts, allowed to grow and thrive, killing over seven million people before Allied powers finally brought an end to the insanity.

It's impossible to make sense of what happened at the death camps. That knowledge comes only from the One who created us. But if there is a lesson for us, perhaps it's a message of intolerance. Intolerance for senseless human suffering. Suffering we must never turn our backs on. To do so would degrade our morality, making us no better than the ancient Romans who derived pleasure from the senseless massacre of Christians in the Coliseum.

In scripture, Saint James tells us we must always be vigilant and confront evil in this world.

> For one who knows the right thing to do and does not do it, it is a
> sin. (James 4:3-4)

I pray God gives us the vision to recognize the truth, and the courage to always do what is right, regardless of the cost.

What I saw here will remain a part of me, the eyes of the damned forever etched in my mind. But beyond the darkness, I leave here with a greater understanding of the true depth of human misery. It has put my own trials and challenges in a different light. As I confront adversity in my life, I hope I endure it with the same dignity and courage as those who perished here.

In the Book of Revelation, John poetically described the vision and imagery of His return. It is his words that give me comfort and solace, knowing in the end, pain and suffering in the world will no longer exist.

> He will wipe every tear from their eyes and there shall be no more
> death or mourning, wailing, or pain for the old order has passed.

The End

CROSSCURRENTS
EVANGELIZING A MODERN AGNOSTIC CULTURE

Eugene P. Trager

> One of the twelve disciples, Thomas (called the Twin), was not with them when Jesus came. So the other disciples told him, "We have seen the Lord!" Thomas said to them, "Unless I see the scars of the nails in his hands and put my finger on those scars and my hand in his side, I will not believe." A week later the disciples were together again indoors, and Thomas was with them. The doors were locked, but Jesus came and stood among them and said, "Peace be with you." Then he said to Thomas, "Put your finger here, and look at my hands; then stretch out your hand and put it in my side. Stop your doubting, and believe!" Thomas answered him, "My Lord and my God!" Jesus said to him, "Do you believe because you see me? How happy are those who believe without seeing me." (John 20:24-31)

In recent years, there has been an effort by biblical scholars such as John Dominic Crossan, Marcus Borg, Bishop Robert Barron, Andrew Newberg, and Eugene D'Aquili to provide interpretations of scripture that would appeal to modern highly educated, scientifically minded agnostic people in our secular culture who live on the fringe of our religious traditions. This is a rather unique evangelistic strategy. The problem with such an approach according to Cardinal John Henry Newman is that in order to be evangelized, people need to believe in something that cannot be apprehended by the senses or understood by reason.

(Apologia 1865-Chapter 5)

That's a problem for modern agnostics. This article examines the evangelizing efforts of Crossan, Borg, Barron, Newberg and D'Aquili in their attempt to deal with this problem.

Borg and Crossan begin by focusing on the epistles attributed to St. Paul and the text of Acts. They point out that Paul's epistles to the churches he established make up over one-fourth of the New Testament, that he is considered the greatest missionary in Church history and that without him there would not be Christianity as we know it. Therefore to address the agnostic's doubt, evangelization must begin with Paul.

First, in trying to make Paul appeal to modern agnostics Borg and Crossan emphasize that Paul was transformed from a radical egalitarian champion of democracy and freedom for all, including slaves, women and the poor, to a conservative defender of the status quo by others writing or editing in his name.[1] Clearly this is an appeal to the liberal political sentiments of modern agnostics:

> There is neither Jew nor Greek, there is neither slave nor free,
>
> There is no male and female, for you all are one in Christ Jesus: (Galatians 3:28)

But then:

> Slaves, obey your earthly masters with respect and fear, and with sincerity of heart, just as you would obey Christ. (Ephesians 6:5-8)
>
> Everyone must submit to governing authorities. For all authority comes from God, and those in positions of authority have been placed there by God. (Romans 13:1)
>
> I do not permit a woman to teach or to assume authority over a man, she must be quiet. (Timothy 2:12)

Second, they point out that the problem with the biblical account of Paul's trip to Damascus was that he could not have been empowered with authority from a high priest in Judea to go to Damascus to arrest dissident Jewish followers of Jesus, and bring them back to Jerusalem for punishment, because a Jewish high priest in Judea could never exercise authority across Roman provincial borders, especially as far away as Damascus.[2] More likely, they imply, Paul went to Damascus, his old stomping grounds where he was educated, to ally himself with his former Jewish colleagues, the members of the Damascus synagogue where he received his Pharisaic education, in order to develop a strategy for punishing members of the Jewish Jesus sect. This alternative explanation appeals to the modern agnostic's concern about scripture's legal and historical inaccuracy and provides a more credible explanation.

Third, and more compelling, Crossan and Borg suggest that when Paul became involved with the Jesus sect in Damascus, his hostility to them began to dissipate as he was emotionally drawn into their ecstatic faith in Jesus' resurrection, and their comradery and love for one another. It was in this state of emotional and religious ecstasy that he experienced his famous vision of Jesus in the city of Damascus.[3] Why is this alternative interpretation more compelling to modern agnostics? Agnostics have always been skeptical about the Biblical versions of Paul's vision of Jesus on the road to Damascus. (Acts 9:4-5, 22:6-21, 26:26) For scientifically minded modern agnostics, Crossan and Borg's version of Paul's religious conversion has a certain plausible resonance.

There is considerable scientific evidence from neurology that our brains are wired such that in intense emotional and ecstatic states, we can and do experience visions especially of people who are important to us. These are not the hallucinations experienced by those in psychotic states or in states of extreme anxiety. Such hallucinations are primarily auditory and due to abnormal neural pathways in diseases such as schizophrenia and bipolar disorder.

Consider Season 2, Episode 22 of the popular television series "The West Wing" entitled "Two Cathedrals" and Season 3 Episode 1 & 2. The President of the United States, Josiah Bartlet, is deciding whether to run for a second term in the midst of a deluge of unfavorable publicity. He is sitting alone in his office in an intense state of grief over the unexpected and sudden death in a car accident of his long time personal assistant whom he has known since he was a teenager when she was his high school teacher. He has just returned from her funeral. Suddenly she appears to him in a vision and tells him, if he doesn't run because he is afraid to lose, she doesn't want to know him. He decides to run.

Many liberal agnostic viewers, including the writer of the series, Allan Sorkin who by his own admission is not religious,[4] have taken these episodes to heart, identified with the characters and accepted President Bartlet's vision of his dead personal assistant. Perhaps they have pondered why our brains are wired for such visions, wondered what purpose they serve and who is responsible for the wiring. Perhaps some have dared to think it could be God.

Bishop Robert Barron is known throughout the world for his series World on Fire Catholic Ministries. His capacity to dialogue with atheists, agnostics, Christians, Muslims, Jews, believers, and non-believers is legion. His unique style of evangelism doesn't stray too far from Catholic dogma, yet at the same time provides alternative interpretations of scripture and new ways of contemplating God.

Consider this sympathetic definition of modern agnosticism which Fr. Barron includes in his Words on Fire Study Program Workbook, The Mystery of God: Who God is and Why He Matters:

> In addition to the two phenomena of religion and anti-religion, a further basic orientation is found in the growing world of agnosticism, people to whom the gift of faith has not been given, but who are nevertheless on the lookout for truth, searching for God. Such people do not simply assert: "There is no God." They suffer from his absence and yet are inwardly making their way towards him, inasmuch as they seek truth and goodness.
>
> Pope Benedict XVI, "Address of His Holiness Benedict XVI at the Meeting for Peace in Assisi," October 27, 2011

Aside from God's existence, modern agnostics have two doubts about God's nature. First, they are skeptical of the anthropomorphic depiction of God in scripture and elsewhere, and second, they question the notion of a personal God who looks after us. With the advent of Quantum Physics, some agnostics have pondered the existence of a non-material realty to which Quantum Physics points, and wondered if God exists in in this reality. Perhaps they hope that in some distant future, science will find out.

In his workbook, The Mystery of God: Who God is and Why He Matters, Fr. Barron takes these issues head on. "While different creatures are ordered to different ends, and thus have different essences, what they have in common is that none of them has to exist. There could be a world without fish, or birds, or stars, or even people. But God is different. God is the being whose *essence is existence*. God is not one being in the universe, or even a being who exists outside of the universe in a special realm. Instead God just is 'existence,' or in the words of Pope St. John Paul, 'the great Existent.'"[5] Barron goes on to emphasize that God is not a being in the universe (or outside the universe) that can be discovered through scientific investigation because he is Being itself. While this rather unique definition, which doesn't stray too far from Catholic Dogma, may appeal to modern agnostics and allow them to accept God's existence on those terms, believers will wonder how Fr. Barron concludes that the creator of the universe is a personal God who is concerned with us, a conclusion that is very important to them. Here, Fr. Barron relies on Pope John Paul II and the Catechism of The Catholic Church:

On October 22, 1996, John Paul II speaking to the members of the Pontifical Academy of Science in plenary assembly stated, "I would remind you that the spiritual soul is created directly by God. Our spiritual soul refers to our intellect and free will. It does not come about from evolutionary processes as does our body and cannot be explained by neurophysiological processes. Scripture suggests metaphorically that God Breathed life into man (Genesis 2:7) and that is why we have God like attributes like intellect, free will and rationality."

As the Catechism of the Catholic Church tells us, "The soul, the seed of eternity we bear in ourselves, is irreducible to the merely material, and can have its origin only in God."[6] Thus to the extent that our soul is linked to eternity which is non material and is shared with God, so it is that God of necessity takes a personal interest in us and loves us, a view that Thomas Nagel, a contemporary agnostic philosopher says we should give serious consideration.[7]

Andrew Newberg and Eugene D'Aquili using state of the art SPECT[8] scans and radioactive tracer isotopes that lock on to brain cells, examined the brains of meditating Buddhists and Franciscan nuns at prayer. They discovered that intensely focused spiritual contemplation alters the circuitry of the brain so that a person perceives transcendent religious experiences as occurring outside the self. Newberg and D'Aquili conclude that the sensation that Buddhists call "oneness with the universe" and the Franciscans call the presence of God is not a hallucination or a delusion or but a chain of neurological events that can be observed, recorded and photographed.[9] It would appear that indeed God is hard-wired into the human brain. Is religion then simply a product of biology? Newberg and D'Aquili have demonstrated the neurophysiological concomitants of the human experience of God. However, they are unable to explain the essence of a soul that is mysteriously linked to a God whose ultimate essence is beyond human comprehension. Despite the unique evangelistic efforts of Crossan, Borg Barron, Newberg, and D'Aquili, the problem that Cardinal Newman identified persists: in order to be evangelized people need to believe in something that cannot be apprehended by the senses or understood by reason. Science and reason can take us pretty far but, ultimately, like Peter, we have to get out of the boat.

Notes

1. Borg, Marcus and John Dominic Crossan, *The First Paul: Reclaiming the Radical Vision* (New York, NY: HarperCollins, 2009), pp 1-2.
2. Borg and Crossan, op. cit., pp. 70-1
3. Crossan, John Dominic, *What really Happened to Paul on the Road to Damascus*, Huff Post, 3/21/2012/Updated 12/6/2017
4. Haught, Nancy, *Religion, Politics Mix in 'West Wing*, 'Orlando Sentinel, March 24, 2001.
5. Barron, Fr. Robert E. and Trent Horn, *The Mystery of God: Who God is and Why He Matters* (Skokie, IL: Word on Fire Catholic Ministries, 2015), pp. 7-8.
6. *Catechism of the Catholic Church*, Second Edition (New York, NY: Doubleday, 1995), p. 20.
7. Nagel, Thomas, *Mind and Cosmos* (New York, NY: Oxford University Press, 2012), pp. 3-12.
8. Single photon emission computed tomography.
9. Newberg, Andrew, and Eugene D'Aquili, *Why God Won't Go Away* (New York, NY: Ballantine Books, 2001), pp. 1-10.

CROSSCURRENTS

GAY MEN, THE INVENTION OF ECCLESIAL INJUSTICE, AND ASPIRATIONS FOR REDRESS AND RENEWAL

Joseph N. Goh

The 2019 progress report of the Sustainable Development Goals states that despite notable developments registered in global efforts towards attaining gender equity (SDG5), these efforts are hampered and undermined by "insufficient progress on structural issues ... such as legal discrimination, unfair social norms and attitudes, decision-making on sexual and reproductive issues and low levels of political participation."[1] The understanding of gender equity in many parts of the world, however, is ordinarily limited to purposeful provisions for the sexual and gender empowerment of women and girls. For instance, the intended reforms in accordance with SDG5 in Malaysia—whence the case studies on gay men for this article are drawn—concentrate solely on female citizens in terms of the eradication of discrimination, violence, sexual exploitation, forced marriages and female genital mutilation (FGM), redressing unpaid reproductive labor, inaccessibility to leadership and ownership positions in socio-political and economic arenas, and attenuated accessibility to resources pertaining to technology as well as sexual and reproductive health and rights.[2]

While these reforms are indispensable in the pursuit of greater equity in Malaysia that is home to 32.6 million people,[3] I argue that they ironically demonstrate a lack of inclusivity on numerous levels through a deliberate elision of lesbian, gay, bisexual, transgender and queer (LGBTQ) issues.[4] Malaysian leaders portray LGBTQ people as enemies of Islam, consumers of a deviant and immoral culture, satanic disciples, malady-stricken miscreants, and hapless victims of western moral depravity.[5] They dismiss LGBTQ rights, principally same-sex marriages, as antithetical to Malaysian values[6] despite the fact that sexually diverse and gender-variant people are an indelible part of the history of the Malay Archipelago.[7]

Same-sex expressions are criminalized in both secular and *Syariah* (Islamic) laws.[8] Protection against gender discrimination as enshrined in Article 8(2) of the Federal Constitution has been interpreted as exclusive of sexual diversity and by extension, gender variance as both non-normative genders and sexualities are often conflated.[9] For instance, gay men are sometimes perceived as obsessively desirous of Gender Affirming Surgeries and transgender women are accused of being men who merely impersonate women.

State-sanctioned exclusion of LGBTQ people is not executed exclusively in Malaysian politics and jurisprudence, but also in non-affirming ecclesial spaces. Akin to Malaysia's deliberate focus on women and girls in its SDG5 advocacies, such churches readily embrace and support gender-related social justice issues, insofar as they represent "decent" and "respectable" heteronormative and cisnormative issues, such as those involving women and girls who conform to socio-culturally sanctioned gender performativities. These efforts are undeniably crucial but deficient in ecclesial efforts towards more holistic gender equity in the country. Fueled by one-dimensional approaches to biblical interpretation, tradition and canonical legalities, non-affirming churches stand as unyielding bastions that participate in the ossification of what the United Nations refers to as "structural issues" of inequity which contribute to suspicion and discrimination among LGBTQ people.

In this article, I showcase narratives from Malaysian Christian gay men that evince the injustice they experience in their own churches and their hopes for a more affirming praxis of communal Christianity in the country. "Aadesh," "Artisan," "Freddie," "Henri" and "Rainbowboy", whose selected narratives I feature, are English-speaking, educated, self-identifying gay men of various Christian denominations from Malaysia's Klang Valley who participated in a more expansive qualitative research project I undertook between 2012 and 2014 involving thirty Malaysian gay and bisexual men.[10] While some of them continue to attend church services, others have ceased any form of ecclesial participation and formulated individualized spiritualities or combined both, as most churches continue to act as sites of protracted oppression, intolerance and stigmatization for Christians whose sexual and gender identities are incongruous with ecclesial and theological heteronormativity and cisnormativity. I am not setting out to construct a gay-affirming or masculinist ecclesiology in this article, or generalize the experiences of Malaysian gay men. My intention is to accompany the discourses of a selection of Malaysians who are customarily silenced and disregarded due to condescending perceptions of aberrance and iniquity by unpacking the praxis of ecclesial prejudice to which they are subjected and their imaginings of radical inclusivity in their own faith communities. The realities of these gay men resonate with other LGBTQ people in and beyond Malaysia.

Despite the many important inroads that governments and churches worldwide have made in terms of LGBTQ affirmation, including in Asia, these efforts continue to be the exception rather than the norm.[11] By showcasing the voices of Asian people who live in Asia, I wish to provide a reminder of these extant realities as well as augment mostly Western-slanted literature on the continuing discomfiture and tension that exist between LGBTQ Christians and their churches due to non-normative sexualities and genders, and struggles with issues of heterosexism and heteropatriarchy.[12] As such, *my goal in this article is to unpack the main dynamics of ecclesial injustice as encountered by gay men, and parse the meanings behind their hopes for redress and eventual change on the part of churches*. In some ways, these hopes can be interpreted as a desire for "reparative justice," or "a certain set of meanings that are communicated between those who make amends and those who receive them."[13] Rather than (re)entrenching them as victims devoid of agency or self-actualization, I aim to expose and foreground the real challenges that these men face and their aspirations for more life-giving ecclesial futurities.

I use the term "ecclesial injustice" in this article to refer to church practices, policies and programs which seek to obliterate, denounce or stifle same-sex attractions and behaviors which depart from acceptable gender norms and expectations. "Affirming" and "radical inclusivity" point towards "an attitude of total and unconditional acceptance"[14] of LGBTQ people instead of conditional acceptance or patient tolerance.

Devising injustice

In Muslim-majority Malaysia, Christianity—along with Buddhism, Hinduism and other non-Muslim faiths—is a minority religion. Christians comprise Roman Catholics, Orthodox Catholics, Anglicans, Lutherans, Methodists, Baptists and Presbyterians, in addition to members of the Salvation Army, Assembly of God, Full Gospel Tabernacle and Evangelical Free Church.[15] These are but a smattering of Christian traditions that have proliferated in Malaysia since the sixteenth century with the notable arrival of Roman Catholicism.[16] With the exception of Good Samaritan Kuala Lumpur (GSKL) and Antioch Mission in Asia (AMA) which mostly command membership of lesbian and gay Christians, and are unrecognized by both state and mainstream Malaysian Christian hierarchies,[17] churches in Malaysia generally decry same-sex behaviors and unions.[18]

Consequently, many gay men have abandoned a Christian identity and/or church affiliation and/or participation, often in rage and sorrowful disillusionment with the contradiction they perceive between the proclamation of an affirming God, and conditional acceptance or outright rejection by churches. Unfortunately, "for too many Christians today, their belief in God who is forgiving and inclusive is challenged by a church which is not forgiving and inclusive."[19] Some continue to participate in religious events but compartmentalize their religious and sexual identities. Others embrace celibacy with mixed emotions. Others still construct distinctions between church and God, and formulate individualized spiritualities that are premised on a mélange of scriptural interpretation, traditional practices and non-Christian elements, and which eschew or minimize any form of ecclesial affiliation or adherence to doctrinal stipulations.[20] There is a significant number of Christian gay men, however, for whom individualized practices of Christianity that are devoid of church affiliation and/or participation do not constitute the fullness of a Christian identity. When I asked Artisan, a Cantonese-Chinese Malaysian and Pentecostal Christian in his late forties on how he felt about church in regard to in his relationship with God, he responded as such:

> It's part of my life. I wouldn't say it's an option. And when I say I'm a Christian, one way to show your love is to be in a fellowship of his family, the brothers and sisters, instead of, oh God can be

everywhere, but if you can be outside, we don't have to go to church or whatever, I don't think this is a relationship.

Christianity, as Artisan envisions it, is a communal rather than personal practice which is suitably expressed through active performances of fellowship with "[God's] family" by "going to church" rather than a solitary devotion that hinges on a belief in God's omnipresence. Sathianathan Clarke posits that "Asian theology is personal but not private,"[21] and its living out for many is communally exercised. For Artisan, a relationship with God is significantly compromised without regular church attendance. Artisan's view represents many sexually diverse and gender-variant Christians in the country for whom the doings of faith are necessarily annexed to, if not conflated with church participation, even if they have experienced churches as sites of oppression. The narratives in the ensuing section unveil the highly nuanced and intricate details of structural sexual inequity which contribute to ecclesial injustice.

Remedying homosexuality

Among the many manifestations of such injustice, Christian gay men speak most passionately against attempts at reparative therapy, also known as conversion or aversion therapy, which "is rooted in the notion that any nonheterosexual sexual orientation is a pathology in need of a 'cure'"[22] but "challenged in court and found to be a fraud perpetrated on LGBTQ people and their families."[23] Freddie, a Hokkien-Chinese Malaysian educator in his early thirties who calls himself a "liberal Christian" recounts an experience of reparative therapy in the form of gay exorcism by well-meaning church leaders at his former church:

> I had demons. At one point they sat me in the middle of a sanctuary, pastors and senior leaders of one of my former churches, they sat me in the middle of the sanctuary and they were arranged surrounding me like a circle, and they started to pray in tongues and started to cast demons out of me, and started to pray for the blood of Jesus to cover me again, and to cleanse me, to heal me from inside out and things like that.

Freddie's detailed account of the exaggerated ritual undertaken by "pastors and senior" leaders to rid him of "demons" through the practice of "pray[ing] in tongues" alludes to three significant ideas concerning individuals with same-sex attraction in many Malaysian churches. First, and not unlike the belief of many churches around the globe, homosexuality is believed to be caused by destructive and debilitating diabolical elements that have successfully entrenched themselves in an individual.[24] Second, same-sex tendency is perceived as an ailment that can be effectively treated and resolved through specific forms of communal prayer that evoke "the blood of Jesus"—a biblical semiotic of "covenant, reconciliation, cleansing, sanctifying, redeeming, justifying, and victory"[25]—as an insulating, protective, cleansing and healing force. Third, churches have also become significant purveyors and mechanisms of a belief that genders and sexualities are reform-able through divine interventions. In so doing, churches become co-conspirators in nation-wide projects of reparative therapy that exist in various pseudo religio-scientific forms. These projects, which mostly involve Malay-Muslim men and occur in dedicated centers,[26] have now found new homes in Malaysian churches.

Rainbowboy, a 22-year-old Cantonese-Hakka-Chinese Malaysian Lutheran has also been exposed to attempts at reparative therapy at a Pentecostal church he is currently attending although his experiences have not been as melodramatic as those of Freddie's:

> They actually have leaders there to talk to you about your sexual orientation, they will have prayer meetings, discussion, counselling, and I think it's what they call to try to make you straight. I mean they don't actually force you to change your orientation. They will tell you to go at that place where you're comfortable with, and if you should really decide for help to be straight again, then by all means you can approach the church leaders, then they could have some sort of prayer meetings or stuff for you.

Rainbowboy speaks of a "comfortable" and conducive environment that is created at his church for gay men like himself who wish to "seek help to be straight again". The mention of the word "again" suggests that these "church leaders" believe in an a priori heterosexual existence, perhaps alluding to an original state of grace that was subsequently tarnished and distorted through the sinfulness of human nature whereby "desire has functioned as an interpretation of the Fall of humanity."[27] Furthermore, one is not "force[d] … to change [one's] orientation," but encouraged to contemplate one's same-sex inclinations in a "place where [one is] comfortable." Many gay men of faith, and other sexually diverse and gender-variant people who cherish their religious beliefs, often construct spaces of spiritual breathability in response to experiences of homophobia, transphobia and biphobia in churches.

I argue that the comfortable place of which Rainbowboy's church leaders speak is in reality an avenue to unnerve and destabilize any form of self-assurance and self-actualization that has transpired in Christian gay men who may have established an interior reconciliation between their sexuality and spirituality, and who are learning to understand that both elements of subjectivity "are flip sides of each other—to be sexual is to be spiritual; and to be spiritual is to be sexual."[28] I suggest that for these leaders, the very notion of being Christian while remaining gay is unthinkable.

In contrast with Freddie's experience, Rainbowboy's is subtle. Rather than an explicit and elaborate ceremony of exorcism, a gay man is subtly invited to self-reflection and subsequently the possibility of ostensibly non-threatening "prayer meetings, discussion[s and/or] counselling" through which a transformation in sexual desire can potentially occur. Reparative therapy is thus couched in persuasively palatable and pastoral terms. The creation of such options denotes a belief that homosexuality is a divinely disapproved passing phase that should be tolerated at best. Thus, while the presence of a gay man may even be embraced at church, his sexual proclivities can never be accepted or affirmed. The sinner is loved, but his "sins" must continue to be decried and his condition "cured."

Persecuting from the pulpit

Some Malaysian gay men may not be subjected to reparative therapy, but still experience verbal attacks on their sexualities from their church leaders. Henri, a 30-year-old self-described "liberal Anglican" Tamil-Indian Malaysian deplores the malice that is embedded in "sermons":

> When you go to church and there's sermons that, you've got the preacher, the minister, saying things, having his outburst against homosexuality out of nowhere, or making other sorts of statements, I just feel like, why do I want to subject myself to this, I'm going to church, and I almost invariably leave being more

frustrated than I was before I went in, yeah, I don't need this and I don't think this is me.

The "outburst" which Henri mentions refers to his righteous rage which erupts upon hearing "sermons"—likely shorter Anglican homilies—that bemoan a perceived moral decadence in the country. While this type of religious rancor rails primarily against "homosexuality," it also targets departures from gender norms and expectations involving the role of Malaysian women as homemakers.[29] The pedagogical act of speaking against sexually diverse and gender variant people from the pulpit conscripts a God who is partisan to and solely favorable of heteronormative and cisnormative agendas, and protracts an incitement to homophobia, transphobia and biphobia in the country.

Henri's motivation for "going to church" is likely for the experience of God's unequivocal acceptance through a performance of communal liturgies and interactions which "envisions not only the creation of a church in which LGBT Christians are beloved, but a church in which all Christians, of all sexualities, can grow into fullness of life by the grace of God."[30] Nonetheless, he discovers that the reality is quite the reverse for him. Based on his experience, church effectively canonizes condemnation, and his statements that he "do[es]n't need this and … do[es]n't think this is [him]" instantiates a firm refusal to "subject [him]self" repeatedly to a potential guilt-induced sense of anti-gay victimhood at his (former) church.

Artisan shares similar experiences of what Michael Bernard Kelly calls "structured, sanctified oppression"[31] at "mainline churches," or churches which propound conservative, non-affirming theological approaches to LGBTQ people and practices:

> Even though the mainline churches have been preaching it over the pulpit, you know, Sunday after Sunday, on their sermons that gay is sinful, gay go to hell and all that, I don't believe it. I used to be scared about it and that's why I stop having sex with men for a long time … but now, with my personal relationship with God, coming to know more gay pastors and all that, and through our conversation, their teachings and all that, I don't think I am excluded from the love of God.

The "public excoriation of non-heteronormative sexuality … typical in many churches"[32] which Artisan used to experience on a weekly basis propels him towards a self-imposed abstinence from "having sex with men" due to a deep-seated fear of offending God and the prospect of eternal damnation. For a period of time, he interiorized an ecclesial ideology that being a non-celibate gay man "excluded [him] from the love of God" as being sexually active contradicts common ecclesial exhortations for sexually diverse and gender-variant people to desist from acting on their inclinations.[33] Nevertheless, due to his "personal relationship with God," or the formulation of a gay-affirming individualized spirituality that lies beyond the prescription and policing of "mainline churches," he now finds himself liberated from his previous fears and included in God's loving acceptance.

Artisan's spiritual turnabout is also invigorated by steady acquaintance and interaction with "gay pastors," possibly those whom he has met at open and affirming ecclesial spaces and/or events in and outside the country. Openly gay male pastors of Asian descent who are also human rights activists include Joe Pang and Jason Ho of Hong Kong,[34] Gary Chan and Miak Siew of Singapore, Joseph Chang of Taiwan, and Patrick S. Cheng and Boon Lin Ngeo of the United States. The presence of gay Christian pastors does not only endorse what is frequently condemned as blasphemous and unacceptable interlacings of faith and non-normative sexualities and genders. That pastors—representatives of God and church who are dedicated to interpreting, exercising, upholding and proclaiming divinely revealed truths—can be radically self-appreciating gay men themselves amplifies Artisan's self-validation as a Christian gay man and fractures the myth that a Christian identity is necessarily heteronormative and cisnormative.

In experiences of "entrenched, sanctified homophobia"[35] from—and perhaps extending beyond—the pulpit that are similar to those of Henri's and Artisan's, 41-year-old Malayalee-Indian Malaysian Aadesh who identifies as a non-practicing Roman Catholic attributes his previous decision of withholding his sexuality from public knowledge to the operations of churches:

> One of the reasons I think I was in the closet for so long was because of my faith. Here was a church that's saying that inherently there's something wrong with you. After I came out, I never doubted God but there was a clear rejection, in sort of like you

know don't hurt me anymore, because … you've kept me in the closet for long enough.

Unlike Freddie and Artisan, Aadesh demonstrates a conflation of God and church in his perception of the faith. Despite the fact that he "never doubted God" and thus understands that "God cannot be used as the excuse to exclude women, gay, lesbian, bisexual, transgendered [sic] or other marginalized people,"[36] the "clear rejection" that he experienced at his previous church was inevitably translated as God's own repudiation of his sexuality. Roman Catholicism paints a condescending image of people with same-sex attraction as miserable unfortunates in need of "respect, compassion, and sensitivity,"[37] their tendencies as "objectively disordered"[38] and their sexual activities as gravely depraved, intrinsically disordered, contravening natural law, futile, and lacking true anatomical and emotional complementarity.[39]

What many non-affirming Christian establishments do not realize is that sexuality is integral rather than peripheral to the subjective production of many gay men, just as both sexuality and faith—"which seem to touch the very core of a person—the soul even"[40]—are integral to the subjective production of many Christian gay men. Hence, the "trial"[41] which Roman Catholicism is convinced that people with same-sex attraction endure does not stem from non-normative sexuality itself, but from political, socio-cultural and religious antagonism towards sexual tendencies which people with same-sex attraction experience as innate and a variation of human sexuality rather than pathological and sinful. As such, to be rebuffed through this logic by churches as representatives of God is for Aadesh's very existence to be devalued and dismissed by God.

During the course of our conversation, Aadesh explained that being "in the closet" for him was not as much a matter of concealing his sexual identity in the public sphere as it was an active practice of denying who he really was to himself. He appears to perceive "'outness' as a reflection of a positive identity,"[42] and to remain "in the closet" or eschew any form of self-acceptance is thus a deliberate act of shameful self-diminishment due to a reiterated and an interiorized belief in his worthlessness in the sight of God as ratified by the church's pronouncement that "there's something wrong with [him]." Little wonder therefore that even after Aadesh is able to embrace his sexuality, the sensation of being smothered by his faith lingers in an indefinite manner. Emotionally-tagged memories of being "hurt" by Christianity continues to deliver an incapacitating experience.

Imagining redress and renewal

This section explores the narratives in which some of the gay men I interviewed articulate their hopes for churches to make amendments and undergo change in relation to their treatment of gay men by non-affirming Malaysian churches. These hopes, I suggest, are also aspirations for reparative justice. While Christian leaders and churches in various parts of the world have apologized for acrimonious attitudes towards LGBTQ people in both unambiguous and tentative tones,[43] no such endeavor exists in Malaysia. On the contrary, subtle measures to stamp out sexual diversity and gender variance have increased in recent years.[44] The following narratives are some responses from my research participants to my question on what they want to hear churches say to them in connection to their sexuality. For Rainbowboy, nothing short of a radically inclusive ecclesial demeanor is acceptable:

> I would prefer, they will actually like, tell that to all the people, to gays like us that it's okay to be gay and it's okay to be Christian at the same time. Sometimes I really like the church to be more supportive for us, to actually tell us that it's okay to be gay. Just come to the church. Everyone is fine with it, we're your friends, we don't judge you, and yeah, we just want to get along with you.

A pronouncement from churches that "it's okay to be gay and ... Christian at the same time" is, as Rainbowboy understands it, simultaneously an official declaration of unqualified affirmation for Christian gay men. He translates his earnest hope for churches to act in an unconditionally "supportive" manner towards gay men as the extension of genuine, heartfelt friendship and fellowship, and the absence of vituperative judgement. An invitation to "just come to church" is simultaneously an invitation to be part of a Christian community without what must often seem as an obligatory accompanying experience of suspicion, secrecy, subterfuge and skepticism.

A church where "everyone is fine with it"—"it" being shorthand for being gay—is the provision of a communal space where gay men's sexualities and spiritualities can be openly acknowledged, celebrated and shared as mutually constructive and enriching. Redress and renewal must thus be a radical reversal of, as George Zachariah observes, how "sanctuaries which are expected to offer hospitality, comfort, and fellowship to all those who are weary and heavy-laden have become places that breed hatred, prejudice, and bigotry"[45] for people of non-normative genders and sexualities.

Henri appears to be doubtful of unconditional affirmation as materializations of redress and renewal, but expresses what he deems as acceptable:

> Ultimately what I would like to hear is you're welcome to this church, that God loves you as you are, but failing that I would settle for not being vilified, not being made to feel that you are an anomaly, or rather that I'm an aberration to the natural order of things, yeah. That would be the least I could hope for.

The fundamental message that Henri desires to hear from churches is that of an unequivocal "welcome" predicated on the principle that "God loves [gay men] as [they] are," and which gestures towards a conviction in God's purposeful creation of gay men,[46] a view similarly held by other sexually diverse and gender-variant Christians.[47] This radical welcome also constitutes radical affirmation as it does not stipulate any condition either for ecclesial membership or pedagogical communications of divine love from churches.

As alluded to earlier, Henri almost seems to envision this approach as idealistic and likely unattainable when he expresses an alternative of "not being vilified" and treated as "an anomaly" or "an aberration to the natural order." This secondary option, a form of "qualified acceptance of homosexuality"[48] serves the purpose of enabling him to be respectfully treated as a fellow Christian insider instead of being reviled as a deviant outsider. Henri appears to be minimally amenable to a situation in which churches are willing to refrain from their liberal and vociferous vilification of gay men as a divine mandate, and merely tolerate him and any expression of his sexuality even if they continue to disagree with how he chooses to live his life and faith. There are, as such, realistic limits to imagining and realizing ecclesial restitution and change.

Not all Christian gay men, however, seek redress and renewal. Churches have lost their significance for Aadesh and his self-understanding as a Christian gay man:

> I've never asked myself that question because I don't believe that it needs to say anything to me anymore. I don't look at the church as playing that function, maybe that's why I identify as a non-practicing Catholic, listen, like many things in the history of the church, our absolutes have often been wrong. I finally have come to a place where I don't need the church to hear that anymore, I would say that because for young people who were like me, who are in church, and who really, genuinely want to be a part of that expression, for their sense of acceptance, that would be important, but not for me anymore.

Aadesh also challenges "an inflated sense of discursive authority"[49] in churches that dismisses the truths of actual lived realities. He speaks back to hubris of churches by bringing to light the reality of mistakes that exist "in the history of the church," including present "absolutes" in understanding and acting on issues of sexual diversity. By highlighting ecclesial errors, Aadesh engages in a "politics of counter-rejection"[50] which challenges and argues against the boastful metanarratives of churches.

Nevertheless, he holds no hope for redress or renewal. For him, churches only play a significant role in the lives of "young people" who continue to appreciate their involvement in church-related activities in order to gain "acceptance." As "a non-practicing Catholic," he purposefully creates a chasm between churches and his sexuality, and renders churches irrelevant and inconsequential to his existence. Aadesh no longer looks to churches for guidance, wisdom, validation or approval for his life as a gay man.

Conclusion

In the experiences of Aadesh, Artisan, Freddie, Henri and Rainbowboy, ecclesial injustice assumes the primary modes of reparative therapy and verbal castigations in churches. As these men and I have discerned together, such dynamics prove to be problematic and oppressive on numerous levels. Churches perpetuate the myth of gay men as demon-infested, psychologically broken beings in need of healing, conversion and repair by way of "heterosexualisation."[51] They insult the capacity of gay men as "morally [and] spiritually bankrupt"[52] subjects to form productive relationships with God, other Christians and fellow human beings. By constructing these men as emblems of deviance, churches unwittingly sustain the notion that gay men are deserving targets of vitriol due to their "sinfulness" and collude with the ongoing systemic vulnerability of sexually diverse and gender-variant communities in Malaysia. Ecclesial injustice is an act of violence by churches against sexually diverse and gender-variant people in the name of a God whom they also paradoxically proclaim as all-embracing and limitlessly inclusive. Some of these men imagine possibilities of redress and renewal from churches in the form of ecclesial repentance and/or greater or wholehearted acceptance. Their musings are reflective of the desire for reparative justice, aware as they are that "the struggle for justice is an expression of faith in a world of injustice."[53] Others like Aadesh are more inclined towards a complete detachment from official ecclesial spaces.

If Malaysian churches are sincere in their mission to be the loving presence of God in the twenty-first century, they need to re-evaluate their existing understanding and practices of inclusivity. If "the Christian faith is about God-human and human-human interconnectedness [and t]he church is a player responsible for fulfilling such interconnectedness,"[54] churches can play an important role in empowering LGBTQ people and assisting them in addressing the fragmentation caused by political, socio-cultural and ecclesial disapprobation. In the context of sexual diversity, the mission of power that churches hold must "[lead] to considerable diversity of expression, growth and human flourishing."[55] Churches need to believe in, appreciate and be committed to deepening their understanding of diverse human realities, an approach which can only serve to shed greater light on the meaning and relevance of their own existence in an ever-evolving world.

Notes

1. United Nations, "Progress of Goal 5 in 2019," Sustainable Development Goal 5: Achieve Gender Equality and Empower All Women and Girls, 2019, https://sustainabledevelopment.un.org/sdg5.
2. Department of Statistics Malaysia, "Sustainable Development Goals Indicators," Sustainable Development Goals, 2015, https://www.dosm.gov.my/v1/uploads/files/4_Portal%20Content/2_%20Statistics/SDG/goals/Goal_5.pdf.
3. Department of Statistics, Malaysia, "Current Population Estimates, Malaysia, 2018-2019," Population & Demography, 2019, https://www.dosm.gov.my/v1/index.php?r=column/ctheme

ByCat&cat=155&bul_id=aWJZRkJ4UEdKcUZpT2tVT090Snpydz09&menu_id=L0phe
U43NWJwRWVSZklWdzQ4TlhUUT09.
4. In this article, I use "LGBTQ" interchangeably with "sexually diverse and gender-variant." I also refer to gay, lesbian and bisexual people as "people with same-sex attraction."
5. Fadly Samsudin, "Jihad Lawan Nafsu Songsang," *Harian Metro*, November 14, 2018, https://www.hmetro.com.my/addin/2018/11/395146/jihad-lawan-nafsu-songsang; Hafidz Baharom, "Najib: LGBTs, Liberalism, Pluralism Are Enemies of Islam," *The Malaysian Insider*, July 19, 2012, http://www.malaysia-today.net/najib-lgbts-liberalism-pluralism-are-enemies-of-islam/; Lazaroo, Suzanne, "Jamil: Govt Programmes Can Help Reduce LGBT Activities," *The Star Online*, March 28, 2016, http://www.thestar.com.my/news/nation/2016/03/28/jamil-govt-programmes-can-help-reduce-lgbt-activities/; Rahimy Rahim, "M'sia Must Not Bow to International Pressure on LGBT Issues, Says Anwar," *The Star Online*, May 15, 2019, https://www.thestar.com.my/news/nation/2019/05/15/msia-must-not-bow-to-international-pressure-on-lgbt-issues-says-anwar/; Teh, Eng Hock, "Dr Puad: LGBT a Treatable Illness," *The Star Online*, January 22, 2013, http://www.thestar.com.my/News/Nation/2013/01/22/Dr-Puad-LGBT-a-treatable-illness/.
6. Kaos, Joseph Jr., "Dr M: M'sia Does Not Accept LGBT Culture, Same-Sex Marriage," *The Star Online*, September 21, 2018, https://www.thestar.com.my/news/nation/2018/09/21/msia-does-not-accept-lgbt-culture-same-sex-marriage/.
7. Farish A. Noor, *What Your Teacher Didn't Tell You: The Annexe Lectures* (Selangor: Matahari Books, 2010), pp. 135-69; Peletz, Michael G., 2006, "Transgenderism and Gender Pluralism in Southeast Asia since Early Modern Times," *Current Anthropology* 47(2), pp. 309-40, https://doi.org/10.1086/498947.
8. The Commissioner of Law Revision, Malaysia, "Federal Constitution" (1957), sec. 377A-C, http://www.agc.gov.my/agcportal/uploads/files/Publications/FC/FEDERAL%20CONSTITUTION%20ULANG%20CETAK%202016.pdf; The Commissioner of Law Revision, Malaysia, "Syariah Criminal Offences (Federal Territories) Act 1997" (2006), sec. 2(1), http://www.agc.gov.my/agcportal/index.php?r=portal2/lom2&id=1431.
9. Mazwin Nik Anis, "Dr Mashitah: No Constitutional Protection for LGBT," *The Star Online*, June 19, 2012, https://www.thestar.com.my/news/nation/2012/06/19/dr-mashitah-no-constitutional-protection-for-lgbt/.
10. Monash University Human Research Ethics Committee Project No. CF12/-2012001355. All pseudonyms and self-descriptions are furnished by the research participants themselves.
11. See Wang, Amber, "#LoveWon: Taiwan Legalises Same-Sex Marriage in Landmark First for Asia," *Hong Kong Free Press*, May 17, 2019, sec. Law & Crime, https://www.hongkongfp.com/2019/05/17/breaking-taiwan-legalises-sex-marriage-landmark-first-asia/; Tong-Kwang Church, "同光同志長老教會 Tong-Kwang Light House Presbyterian Church," 同光同志長老教會, accessed February 27, 2020, https://www.tkchurch.org.
12. See Cornwall, Susannah, 2013, "British Intersex Christians' Accounts of Intersex Identity, Christian Identity and Church Experience," *Practical Theology* 6(2), pp. 220-36, https://doi.org/10.1179/1756073X13Z.0000000001; McQueeney, Krista, 2009, "'We Are God's Children, Y'All:' Race, Gender, and Sexuality in Lesbian- and Gay-Affirming Congregations," *Social Problems* 56 (1), pp. 151-73, https://doi.org/10.1525/sp.2009.56.1.151; Levy, Denise L. and Patricia Reeves, 2011, "Resolving Identity Conflict: Gay, Lesbian, and Queer Individuals with a Christian Upbringing," *Journal of Gay & Lesbian Social Services* 23(1), pp. 53-68, https://doi.org/10.1080/

10538720.2010.530193; Sumerau, J. Edward, 2012, "'That's What a Man Is Supposed to Do,'" *Gender & Society* 26(3), pp. 461-87, https://doi.org/10.1177/0891243212439748; Yip, Andrew K. T., "Sexual Orientation Discrimination in Religious Communities," in *Sexual Orientation Discrimination: An International Perspective*, ed. M. V. Lee Badgett and Jefferson Frank (New York: Routledge, 2007), pp. 209-24.

13. Walker, Margaret Urban, *What Is Reparative Justice?* (Milwaukee, WI: Marquette University Press, 2010), p. 15.

14. Goh, Joseph N., "Practical Guidelines for SOGIESC Theologising in Southeast Asia: Foregrounding Gender Nonconformity, Sexual Diversity and Non-Dyadic Embodiment," in *Siapakah Sesamaku? Pergumulan Teologi Dengan Isu-Isu Keadilan Gender*, ed. Stephen Suleeman and Amadeo D. Udampoh (Jakarta, Indonesia: Sekolah Tinggi Filsafat Theologi Jakarta, 2019), p. 189.

15. Christian Federation of Malaysia, "CFM Components," Christian Federation of Malaysia, 2018, https://cfmsia.org/cfm-components/.

16. Ho, Daniel K. C., "The Church in Malaysia," in *Church in Asia Today: Challenges and Opportunities*, ed. Saphir P. Athyal (Singapore: The Asia Lausanne Committee for World Evangelization, 1996), pp. 257-87.

17. Yubong, Carrey, "Antioch Mission in Asia: Autocephalous (Independent) Church in Catholic Apostolic Tradition," accessed July 18, 2017, http://www.australianchurchofantioch.com/antioch-mission-in-asia.html; Good Samaritan Kuala Lumpur, "Good Samaritan Kuala Lumpur," Facebook, 2020, https://www.facebook.com/gskualalumpur/.

18. National Evangelical Christian Fellowship Malaysia (NECF), "Gay Church: A Response," Berita NECF Articles, December 2007, http://www.necf.org.my/newsmaster.cfm?&menuid=2&action=view&retrieveid=930; Netto, Terence, "Bishop Takes Nuanced Stance on Seksualiti Merdeka," Malaysiakini, November 4, 2011, http://www.majodi.org/index.php/bishop-paul-tan/bishops-desk/129-bishop-takes-nuanced-stance-on-seksualiti-merdeka.

19. Osborne, Kenan B., *A Theology of the Church for the Third Millennium: A Franciscan Approach* (Leiden, The Netherlands: Brill, 2009), p. 375.

20. Yip, Andrew K. T., 2002, "The Persistence of Faith among Nonheterosexual Christians: Evidence for the Neosecularization Thesis of Religious Transformation," *Journal for the Scientific Study of Religion* 41(2), pp. 199-212, https://doi.org/10.1111/1468-5906.00111.

21. Clarke, Sathianathan, "The Task, Method and Content of Asian Theologies," in *Asian Theology on the Way: Christianity, Culture and Context*, ed. Peniel Jesudason Rufus Rajkumar (London: SPCK, 2012), p. 5.

22. Streed, Carl G., et al., 2019, "Changing Medical Practice, Not Patients - Putting an End to Conversion Therapy," *New England Journal of Medicine* 381(6), p. 500, https://doi.org/10.1056/NEJMp1903161.

23. Streed et al., p. 501.

24. Mavhandu-Mudzusi, Azwihangwisi Helen and Peter Thomas Sandy, 2015, "Religion-Related Stigma and Discrimination Experienced by Lesbian, Gay, Bisexual and Transgender Students at a South African Rural-Based University," *Culture, Health & Sexuality* 17(8), 1049-56, https://doi.org/10.1080/13691058.2015.1015614.

25. Young, Adam, 2014, "The Blood of Jesus in Revival Theology and the Contemporary Church with Particular Reference to the East African Revival and Roy Hession," *International*

Journal for the Study of the Christian Church 14(3), p. 303, https://doi.org/10.1080/1474225X.2014.935151.

26. Jade See, "What It Means to Suffer in Silence: Challenges to Mental Health Access among LGBT People (Policy For Action No. 2/ 2019)" (Galen Centre for Health and Social Policy, April 2019), https://galencentre.org/2019/04/22/conversion-therapy-is-a-form-of-violence/; Tham, Jia Vern, "Here's How Malaysia 'Cures' LGBTs With Conversion Therapy," *SAYS.Com*, December 20, 2018, https://says.com/my/news/here-s-how-malaysia-cures-lgbts-with-conversion-therapy.

27. Henderson-Espinoza, Robyn, "Queering Desire," in *Contemporary Theological Approaches to Sexuality*, ed. Lisa Isherwood and Dirk von der Horst (London: Routledge, 2018), p. 125.

28. Yip, Andrew K. T., 2005, "Religion and the Politics of Spirituality/Sexuality," *Fieldwork in Religion* 1(3), p. 276, https://doi.org/10.1558/firn.v1i3.271.

29. Ho, Pauline, "Sibu Declares 2014 as Year of Evangelisation," *Herald: The Catholic Weekly*, December 9, 2013.

30. Garrigan, Siobhan, 2009, "Queer Worship," *Theology & Sexuality* 15(2), p. 229, https://doi.org/10.1558/tse.v15i2.211.

31. Kelly, Michael Bernard, *Seduced by Grace: Contemporary Spirituality, Gay Experience and Christian Faith* (Melbourne, Australia: Clouds of Magellan, 2007), p. 205.

32. Goh, Joseph N., *Living Out Sexuality and Faith: Body Admissions of Malaysian Gay and Bisexual Men* (London: Routledge, 2018), p. 129.

33. Ong, Pauline, "Towards a Responsible and Life-Giving Ministry with and among Sexual and Gender Minorities," in *A Theological Reader on Human Sexuality and Gender Diversities: Envisioning Inclusivity*, ed. Roger Gaikwad and Thomas Ninan (Delhi, India: ISPCK/NCCI, 2017), pp. 333-44.

34. Joe Pang is simultaneously pastoring GSKL.

35. Kelly, *Seduced by Grace*, p. 196.

36. Leung, Josephine, 2010, "A Feminist Cum Queer Reading of Liturgy," *in God's image* 29(3), p. 67.

37. John Paul II, *Catechism of the Catholic Church*, 2nd Ed (E-Book) (Libreria Editrice Vaticana, 1997), para. 2358, http://www.usccb.org/beliefs-and-teachings/what-we-believe/catechism/catechism-of-the-catholic-church/epub/index.cfm.

38. John Paul II, para. 2358.

39. John Paul II, para. 2357.

40. Jakobsen, Janet R. and Ann Pellegrini, *Love the Sin: Sexual Regulation and the Limits of Religious Tolerance*, Sexual Cultures (New York: New York University Press, 2003), p. 99.

41. John Paul II, *Catechism*, para. 2358.

42. Yip, "Religion and the Politics of Spirituality/Sexuality," 285.

43. BBC News, "Pope Francis Says Church Should Apologise to Gay People," *BBC News*, June 27, 2016, sec. Europe, https://www.bbc.com/news/world-europe-36636845; Garrand, Danielle, "Christians Surprise Pride Parade Marchers with Signs Apologizing for Anti-LGBTQ Views," *CBS News*, July 3, 2018, https://www.cbsnews.com/news/christians-surprise-pride-parade-marchers-with-signs-apologizing-for-church-anti-lgbtq-views/; Housden, Victoria, "Tyrone Minister's Church Apology to LGBT Community," *Ulster Herald*, August 2, 2019, sec. Headlines, https://ulsterherald.com/2019/08/02/tyrone-ministers-church-apology-to-lgbt-community/; Michael McGowan, "Perth's Anglican Church Offers 'Heartfelt Apology' to LGBT Community," *The*

Guardian, October 14, 2017, https://www.theguardian.com/world/2017/oct/14/perths-anglican-church-offers-heartfelt-apology-to-lgbt-community.

44. Goh, Joseph N., "A Response to the Talk 'Somewhere Over the Rainbow: Same-Sex Marriage and LGBT' at the Church of the Risen Christ, Kuala Lumpur," *2015,* https://www.josephgoh.org/resources; Goh, Joseph N., "Reflections on the Play 'The Third Way: Same Sex Attraction and the Catholic Church' at Holy Family Church, Kajang," 2015, https://www.josephgoh.org/resources; Goh, Joseph N., "Repent or Believe in the Closet: When Pastoral Care Is Anything But," 2013, https://www.josephgoh.org/resources.

45. Zachariah, George, "Church and Homophobia: Envisioning an Inclusive Church," in *Christian Responses to Issues of Human Sexuality and Gender Diversity: A Guide to the Churches in India*, ed. Philip Kuruvilla (New Delhi & Nagpur, India: ISPCK/NCCI, 2017), p. 13.

46. Harris, Brett, 2018, "Free to Be Me," *CrossCurrents* 68(4), pp. 488-99, https://doi.org/10.1111/cros.12336.

47. Ueno, Reina, 2015, "My Queer Exodus Story: As a Japanese Lesbian Minister in a Rural Church," *in God's image* 34(1), pp. 32-6; Luk, Small, 2015, "God Loves Intersex People," *in God's image* 34(2), pp. 5-13; Wong, Pearl, 2015, "Queering Binary Notions of Sexuality: Proclamation of a Bisexual Feminist," *in God's image* 34(2), pp. 14-24.

48. Zachariah, "Church and Homophobia: Envisioning an Inclusive Church," 9.

49. Goh, Joseph N., "Gender, Sexuality and 'Songsang': Freedom of Expression for LGBT Malaysians?," *Kyoto Review of Southeast Asia* Young Academics Voice, no. 22 (2018), https://kyotoreview.org/yav/gender-sexuality-songsang-freedom-of-expression-lgbt-malaysians/.

50. Yip, Andrew K. T., 1999, "The Politics of Counter-Rejection: Gay Christians and the Church," *Journal of Homosexuality* 37(2), pp. 47-63, https://doi.org/10.1300/J082v37n02_03.

51. Mavhandu-Mudzusi and Sandy, "Religion-Related Stigma and Discrimination Experienced by Lesbian, Gay, Bisexual and Transgender Students at a South African Rural-Based University."

52. Goh, Joseph N., 2017, "Bridging Benedictions, Enlightening Embodiment: Interpretations of Spirit through Desire among Gay and Bisexual Malaysian Men," *Journal for the Study of Spirituality* 7(2), p. 138, https://doi.org/10.1080/20440243.2017.1370907.

53. Russell, Letty M., *Church in the Round: Feminist Interpretation of the Church* (Louisville, KY: Westminster John Knox Press, 1993), p. 123.

54. Leung, "A Feminist Cum Queer Reading of Liturgy," p. 84.

55. Percy, Martyn, *Shaping the Church: The Promise of Implicit Theology* (New York: Routledge, 2016), p. 106.

WASHINGTON GLADDEN AND THE CHRISTIAN NATION

Alfredo Romagosa

This article deals with a question about the United States presented by minister and social reformer Washington Gladden: "The question is sometimes raised whether this is a Christian nation."[1] Of course the answer would depend on what is meant by being a Christian nation. Gladden (1836-1918) is considered to be one of the foundational figures of what came to be known as the Social Gospel movement in the United States. Gladden raises our central question in many ways: "Is this a Christian nation? Does it possess a Christian character? Is its life a Christian life?[2] This is a topic to which he often returns in his many books, and we will discuss his definitions and recommendations in some detail. We will also include references to some of his contemporaries and to later thinkers. One may ask about the relevance of this material in today's world. As the social and religious reality in the United States becomes increasingly complex, many return to the thoughts of the founding fathers for clarifications. But their ideas, heavily influenced by the European enlightenment, were more philosophic than practical. The Social Gospel was the watershed of Christian social thought in the United States, and those interested in the political implications of Christianity for a democratic country should benefit from this analysis.

There are countries where a particular religion is established as the official faith in its constitution. This meaning is clearly disavowed by Gladden: "While we have no desire to see the establishment of any form of religion by law in this land, most of us would be willing to see the nation in its purposes and policies and ruling aims becoming essentially Christian."[3] Can even this limited identity be generally acceptable or practical in the United States today?

The social gospel

Although the term Social Gospel can have a broad scope, a common usage is in reference to a Protestant movement in the United States during the late nineteenth and early twentieth century, and this is our usage in this article. The movement had its roots among Christian groups that had worked for the abolition of slavery, and was influenced by social thinkers from England and Germany. Along with Gladden, other key members of this group that we will discuss were Richard Ely (1854-1943), and Walter Rauschenbusch (1861-1918).

The Social Gospel was not an organized movement with designated leaders or the sponsorship of specific churches. It arose spontaneously from thinkers with different denominational backgrounds. Although it was primarily a Protestant development, there was some positive interaction with the social teachings of the Catholic Church, embodied in the papal social encyclicals. The primary concern of the movement was a dissatisfaction with traditional Christian "charity" or almsgiving, seeking instead real socioeconomic reforms that would improve the actual conditions of the poor and the underprivileged. The influence of this line of thinking declined after World War I. The realities of the war tended to dampen the somewhat idealistic and humanistic themes of the movement, and American Protestantism entered then an era of neo-orthodoxy, returning to a traditional emphasis on personal spiritual salvation. In recent decades, some Social Gospel concerns have been rekindled as a result of economic problems and of the civil rights movement.[4]

Washington Gladden

Washington Gladden was born in 1836 in Pottsgrove, Pennsylvania. His father, who was a school teacher, died when Washington was six, and the boy spent much of his childhood living with his uncle in a farm in Owego, New York.[5] On feeling a call to the ministry in 1855, Gladden began his preparation at the Owego Academy.[6] After finishing his education at Williams College,[7] Gladden was ordained as a minister in 1860 and started his career working in a Congregational church in Brooklyn.[8]

He had assignments at several churches until becoming the pastor of the First Congregational Church in Columbus, Ohio, where he would serve for thirty-two years.[9]

While Gladden was serving at Springfield, Massachusetts (1875-1882), there was a great deal of tension there between labor and capital, due to a long industrial depression and resulting unemployment. Gladden was invited to speak to a group of workers, and he continued with a series of lectures addressed to both workers and employers.[10] After moving to Ohio in 1883 he became even more involved in social issues, since the coal mines of southeastern Ohio were a continuous source of labor conflicts.[11] In addition to his pastoral and lecturing work, Gladden was very active in community and organizational activities. Gladden would go on to write over thirty books on religious and social issues, most of them a result of his preaching and lecturing.

Episcopalian Richard Ely had the advantage of being a trained economist, and he taught this discipline at the University of Wisconsin, John Hopkins University and Northwestern University. Ely studied philosophy and economics at the German universities of Halle, Heidelberg, and Berlin where he was influenced by the German historical school of economic thought.[12] Although Gladden and Ely could be considered to be the most important pioneers of the Social Gospel, and they were obviously aware of each other's work, they were largely independent thinkers. They developed their thought from primarily different sources, Ely from German economists and historians and Gladden from English and American religious authors such as Frederick Robertson and Horace Bushnell.[13] As major contributors to the same cause, however, they met and interacted in a number of congresses and organizations.

Baptist minister Walter Rauschenbusch studied at the Rochester Theological Seminary after attending lectures at several German universities. He acknowledged his debt to the pioneers like Gladden and Ely,[14] but his political ideas were more radical than theirs. He sought significant structural changes in the socioeconomic system of the United States. He was also the most accomplished theologian of the group.

The common good

Gladden's handling of our topic often begins with an important distinction between two sometimes competing aspects within the Christian message: "In the New Testament teaching about conduct two truths are emphasized,—the independence of the individual, the solidarity of society."[15] Different Christian groups have sometimes emphasized one or the other of these aspects through time.

The individual aspect is well established in traditional Christian teaching, as Gladden affirms: "the nature of moral responsibility as personal and individual is clearly affirmed. The fact that guilt and blameworthiness are not transferable; that every man must bear his own burden; that every man must give account of himself unto God...," but he continues, "the solitariness of religious experience must not be denied, but neither must it be unduly magnified. Out of it may easily grow an unholy egoism which is far from the spirit of Christ."[16] Richard Ely adds: "Social solidarity means the oneness of human interests; it signifies the dependence of man upon man, both in good things and in evil things."[17] Clearly, the emphasis on the solidarity or community aspect would be an inherent characteristic of Social Gospel thinking.

This is not an exclusively Christian notion. Human solidarity is the consequence of his social nature, which was been clearly recognized throughout Western civilization, as witnessed by Cicero, "We are not born for ourselves alone, and our country claims her share... in this we ought to take nature for our guide, to throw into the public stock the offices of general utility by a reciprocation of duties... and to cement human society by arts, by industry, and by our resources."[18]

The "corporate" view of human nature is clearly established in the Christian scriptures, including the images of the "Body of Christ" (First Letter of Paul to Corinthians, 12:12-32) and "the Vine and the Branches" (Gospel of John, 15:1-10).

Sociopolitical action

Christian social identity is not just a feeling of shared concern, it is seen to translate into political memberships and responsibilities: "it is a natural organism into which every human being is born; and the duties that pertain to it are no more optional than are our duties to God."[19]

Few would quarrel with the fact that Jesus called his disciples and his church to practice charity, but political actions dealing with specific social problems are more controversial:

> I know that there are some who will promptly say, "No; the nation in this sense is not Christian, and we do not want it to be... The business of a nation is not charity. Its function is not to practice benevolence, but simply to do justice. It ought to keep people from trespassing on one another; it ought to preserve the peace, and provide for the common defense; it ought, so far as possible, to give everyone a chance to exercise his own powers, and there it ought to end."[20]

Regardless of Christian principles, there are many in the United States that would even question the constitutionality of government involvement, at least at the federal level, in socioeconomic programs:

> There is, indeed, in the preamble of the national constitution, one clause which recognizes the duty of the government to 'promote the general welfare', but the implications of that clause have always been disputed; there are many who contend that it is not the nation's business to promote welfare, whether general or special... The prevailing idea of our political science has been that there is no common good, other than liberty, which the nation is organized to promote; that all it has to do is to provide a free arena, in which individuals may compete for such good things as are within their reach. The idea of a large organized co-operation for common ends, through the city or the state or the nation, has been regarded by most as a political heresy.[21]

This question is at the center of many political disputes today. Gladden is clearly on the side of political action to achieve social justice. His argument rests on human inequalities, and the imperfections of any socioeconomic system:

> If all men were born equal in physical and mental equipment; if all were started in the race of life with equal powers and opportunities, this rule of *laissez faire* might be a practicable rule, but it is not so; there are vast inequalities... The truth is that this is a world where compassion must be a constant quantity; there is no kind of human association in which it can be spared; and when the State— that is 'all of us'—undertakes to adjust our human relations, it will not be possible to dispense with compassion.[22]

On the Catholic side, papal teachings have been very emphatic on this issue:

> The foremost duty, therefore, of the rulers of the State should be to make sure that the laws and institutions, the general character and administration of the commonwealth, shall be such as of themselves to realize public well-being and private prosperity... It lies in the power of a ruler to benefit every class in the State, and amongst the rest to promote to the utmost the interests of the poor; and this in virtue of his office, and without being open to suspicion of undue interference—since it is the province of the commonwealth to serve the common good.[23]

The constitutions of many countries are chartered to be more socially proactive than that of the United States. This is not necessarily based on religion, although most religions are supportive of this. The complexities of the political system of the United States are open to controversies on this topic, but there have been enough constitutional rulings so that there is sufficient latitude for government action on social problems. It is the clear contention of the Social Gospel that Christian teachings require an assumption of social responsibility by social orders as well as individuals. Some still use the counter argument that Jesus and his disciples were not politically involved. Gladden addresses this issue:

> The fact that Jesus and his apostles did not deal with social questions in their political aspects may be explained by the fact that those to whom they spoke had no political responsibilities. They were not citizens, they were subjects; to preach politics to them would be like preaching about dancing to people with amputated limbs. If the followers of Jesus had been sovereigns, men clothed with political responsibility, probably he would have had something to say to them about their political duties. The men to whom you and I preach are sovereigns,—the sovereign people; voters in this country are 'the powers that be'; they are ordained of God to organize and administer civil society.[24]

Given the assumption that the Christian has a sociopolitical obligation, there are a number of ways to put this into practice, as we will see in the following sections.

Political leadership

The first component of political responsibility would be to insure the wise selection of leaders: "The Christian is a citizen, and it is part of his Christian duty to see to it that the government is wisely chosen, and that it faithfully performs its duties... There is no better opportunity of doing good than that which presents itself where responsible offices are to be filled."[25]

It is also important to bring civility to the political process, which is particularly applicable in the United States today: "Into this fierce and brutal strife the Christian ought to carry his Christianity; standing always for honor and fair play; for chivalry in the treatment of opponents; for truth and the whole truth against the perversions and concealments of partisans; for all things honest and of good report no matter with what party they may be identified."[26]

And responsibility does not end with election: "The price of liberty and good government is not only eternal vigilance but eternal courage and eternal sacrifice."[27] A critical element wise selections and of "watchfulness" is to be an informed citizen, to take the time to learn about the specific problems of the communities and about the possible solutions: "Let no man speak on these themes who has not qualified himself by careful study; who does not thoroughly know what he is talking about."[28] As an economist and educator, Ely emphasized the importance of detailed socioeconomic knowledge, and he was an important contributor in establishing the study of applied economics in the United States: "Better economic knowledge should bear its fruit in better citizenship. This was the principle which determined the development of the economics department at Wisconsin."[29]

Some Christians are called to further involvement in the actual exercise of leadership roles in political offices, which should be seen as a vocation to service: "Office is not to him a chance for self-aggrandizement or plunder, but a call to consecrated service."[30] In an address to the Congress of the United States in 2015, Pope Francis exhorts this vocational role:

> Your own responsibility as members of Congress is to enable this country, by your legislative activity, to grow as a nation. You are called to defend and preserve the dignity of your fellow citizens in

the tireless and demanding pursuit of the common good, for this is the chief aim of all politics. A political society endures when it seeks, as a vocation, to satisfy common needs by stimulating the growth of all its members, especially those in situations of greater vulnerability or risk. To this you have been invited, called and convened by those who elected you.[31]

Legislation

So far we have dealt with political leadership. When it comes to actual legislation, there was some divergence among Social Gospel thinkers. Gladden and Ely had enough faith in the political system of the United States, that they thought that solutions could be achieved through legislation:

> [Gladden] 'There are many good men, outside the church as well as within it, who believe that the existing social order can never be Christianized; that it must be replaced by a new social system. But most of us are still clinging to the belief that the existing social order can be Christianized, so that justice may be established in it, and good-will find expression through it.'[32]

> [Ely] We must work... to instill Christian principles into our entire public as well as private life... Religious laws are the only laws which ought to be enacted. But what are religious laws? Certainly not in the United States laws establishing any particular sectarian views or any theological tenets, in regard to which there may be diversity of opinion, but laws designed to promote the good life. Factory acts, educational laws, laws for the establishment of parks and playgrounds for children, laws securing honest administration of justice, laws rendering the Courts accessible to the poor as well as the rich- all these are religious laws in the truest sense of the word.[33]

Rauschenbusch, on the other hand, was more pessimistic: "We have an exaggerated idea of the importance of laws... Our zest for legislation blinds us to the subtle forces behind and beyond the law. Those influences which really make and mar human happiness and greatness are beyond the reach of the law."[34] As mentioned above, Rauschenbusch was looking for more radical changes. Nevertheless, he is calling attention to the reform of attitudes that is needed to make possible any kind of social progress. Gladden is aware of this; on dealing with social problems, he calls for the Church to "investigate them and discuss them, till a sound public opinion is created to deal with them."[35]

The public conscience

So far we have discussed some explicit ways in which Christians can act politically, from voting and watchfulness to political office and legislation. But as implied above, there are also more subtle ways of fostering a Christian nation. Gladden spoke of "public opinion," but "public conscience" may be a better term for us to use in that it refers more clearly to issues with a moral content. This is the moral thinking of the majority of the people or perhaps of the most vocal or influential groups. It is a dynamic set constantly affected by events and by the public expressions of leaders from all spheres, including religion, and this is a very fertile field for Christian action. Following on his concern about legislation, Rauschenbusch emphasizes this religious role:

> Religion creates morality, and morality then deposits a small part of its contents in written laws. The State can protect the existing morality and promote the coming morality, but the vital creative force of morality lies deeper. The law becomes impotent if it is not supported by a diffused, spontaneous moral impulse in the community... Thus it is clear that the Church has a large field for social activity before touching legislation.[36]

Ely is more positive:

> The Church can go in many respects far beyond the State. It can place ideals ahead of the State to which the State must gradually approach; it can rebuke and inspire the State; it can quicken the consciences of men, of those who can rule and those who obey. The Church always has the opportunity of doing work neglected by the State... Let all Christians see to it that they put as much as possible, not of doctrine or creed into the State constitution, but of Christian life and practice into the activity of the State.[37]

Civil society

Gladden and other Social Gospel thinkers advocated the explicit actions discussed earlier, but this was easier in their time, when there was a clear majority of practicing Christians in the United States, when many moral issues, such as the rights of the unborn, for example, were seen as fundamental rather than sectarian. The debate on issues relating to gender have also become increasingly complex. This changed situation should not deter the resolve that they advocate, but it makes it more of a challenge. In considering the evolving environment, the current concept of a "civil society" could be helpful.

This is not a new term, and it has been used with different meanings through the centuries, receiving a significant focus during the Scottish Enlightenment, which influenced the early political thinking of the United States. It has come more to the fore after the fall of Russian control, when its former satellites sought guidance in reconstructing democratic ideals. The writings of social philosopher Michael Walzer have been very influential in this area. Commencing from a Jewish viewpoint, Walzer has written extensively on the political role of "intermediate" groups, including religions. What Walzer proposes is essentially a new conceptualization of social organization, including, but distinct from, the political and economic orders. Walzer defines civil society as "the space of uncoerced human association and also the set of relational networks—formed for the sake of family, faith, interest, and ideology—that fill this space."[38] Rather than seeking precision, it is a recognition of the complex and "messy" nature of human society: "The picture here is of people freely associating and communicating with one another, forming and reforming groups of all sorts..."[39]

In contrasts with historical ideologies that overemphasized the state or the economy, the civil society values the intermediate organizations where civility is learned. Not having exclusive power, the different groups, ethnic, religious, or "other," "are free to celebrate their histories, remember their dead, and shape (in part) the education of their children."[40] A key element here is the free association. Gladden had commented on the inconsistency of religious coercion, at least in the context of Christian principles: "we may say that the nation would not be Christian, in the highest and truest sense, if it undertook to enforce by law

Christian beliefs or observances. That would be an infraction of a principle that is fundamental in Christianity. A compulsory faith is a contradiction in terms."[41] Gladden also recognized the value of variety, in spite of the resulting tension:

> In society, as in every other organized existence, beauty and perfection are secured by unity in variety, the harmonious combination of parts that differ... To secure the variety that is desirable, it is well that the individuality of every man and woman be perfectly developed. It is necessary, therefore, to learn how to reconcile these two contending obligations; how to be in society, and not of it; how to respect yourself, your own judgment and conscience, and yet to love your neighbor as yourself; when to withstand the social influences, and when to yield to them.[42]

Religions are by nature absolutizing, since they deal with ultimate realities. But recognizing the limitations of human renderings, there may be some value in religious pluralism. This is not to relativize beliefs, but to clarify them. There have been many attempts to find common moral elements among the world religions, and this can be useful in forging alliances. French philosopher Paul Ricoeur warns of the danger that these efforts may lead to superficiality, to dilutions, but he also recognizes that fundamental principles can sometimes be sharpened by reflecting on the actual contrasts: "We need the atheist so that we can better understand ourselves... We need other religions and their criticisms so as to come out of an excessively interior position."[43]

While admitting the possible value of pluralism, if one is honest, one must recognize that a common ground of beliefs is preferable. But a mixed civil society may be all that is available, and this can work for religious groups if they can truly practice their celebrations, have control over the education of their children, and have some hope of being able to influence the public conscience. But what about groups that advocate policies that may be harmful to the common good? Christians must oppose such policies, not because they come from a specific group, but because they can be shown to be detrimental in the light of a constructively influenced public conscience. This is perhaps an example where Walzer's "messiness" must be acknowledged, and no legitimate religious faith believes that all religions are equally valid. If one believes in one's religion as "good news," one should have confidence on the value of its message in an open forum, both in its inspirational effect and in the beneficial results of applying its teachings about behavior.

Education

The subject of education is worth some discussion. Gladden had some interesting comments on this subject, speaking as a Protestant: "It is the Roman Catholic theory that the work of education belongs to the Church; our American policy entrusts it mainly to the State. Up to a certain point we may adopt the American theory; but it is a grave question whether we have not pushed it quite too far."[44]

Catholics continue to value parochial schools, but economic pressures are mounting, and a number of Protestant groups are beginning to have reflections similar to Gladden's. The United States has an exaggeratedly strict interpretation of the separation of church and state, compared to other countries. Why should a group that wants more control of the education of their children be penalized financially? It would appear that private, religiously affiliated schools can be a vital component of a civil society.

Some states have school voucher programs that provide partial support for private schools, and "charter" schools that have some state regulation but receive less public funding than public schools are becoming more popular. Some of these charter schools are sponsored by religious groups. Questions arise about the practicality of these approaches, but some successful countries, such as Germany, have state-funded religious schools of different denominations. On questions of sizing efficiency, some public schools in the United States are becoming too large for effective management. The potential complications of all these issues should not be ignored, but the deficiencies of the current system also need to be addressed. More pluralism in education would be consistent with the aims of a civil society.

The Kingdom

According to biblical experts, the "kingdom of God" is Jesus' central theme, as He proclaims: "The time is fulfilled, and the kingdom of God is at hand." (Gospel of Mark 1:15) But the kingdom of God, as used by Jesus, does not have a precise definition; it is more of a story or vision. This is often the case with fundamental topics dealing with human life. Verbal definitions fail to capture a vision that is capable of providing the strongest motivation for action. The extensive use of stories and symbols is often more effective. The social gospel thinkers often make use of this theme in their calls for social activism:

> [Gladden:] When we are bidden to seek first the kingdom of God, we are bidden to set out hearts on this great consummation; to keep this always before us as the object of our endeavors; to be satisfied with nothing less than this. The complete Christianization of all life is what we pray for and work for, when we work and pray for the coming of the kingdom of heaven... The kingdom of heaven is the entire social organism in its ideal perfection; the church is one of the organs- the most central and important of them all... society, without those specialized religious functions which are gathered up in the church, would not very readily receive and incarnate and distribute the gifts of the spirit of God.[45]

> [Rauschenbusch] The Kingdom of God is not confined within the limits of the Church and its activities. It embraces the whole of human life. It is the Christian transfiguration of the social order. The Church is one social institution alongside of the family, the industrial organization of society, and the State. The Kingdom of God is in all these, and realizes itself through them all.[46]

In addition to their inspirational contents, both of the above statements anticipated Walzer's concept of the churches being important intermediate organizations, working with and within others, but providing an important "leavening" function. Note that we are not discussing here the various theological interpretations of the concept of the "kingdom," only its symbolic use in our context.

The kingdom of God term had effective appeal in the more faith conscious times of the Social Gospel, but the use of inspirational mottos can still be helpful. Kennedy's *New Frontier* tried to evoke the traditions of the American pioneers. Bush's *Compassionate Conservatism* attempted to be centrist. Unfortunately, partisanship tends to be a serious obstacle although there have been rare but hopeful bipartisan efforts, such as the *Secure America and Orderly Immigration* proposal of senators Kennedy and McCain with its appealing title. There is always a need for inspiration as seen in the message from Reverend J. Brierley, quoted by Gladden: 'What the world really wants... is men who have news from the land of the ideal, who have God's life within them, who open afresh the springs of living water that quench the thirst of the soul.' And Gladden continues:

> But for what kind of news from the land of the ideal are men hungering and thirsting? For the news that brings the ideal down to earth; that makes it no mere dreamy possibility of far-off good, but the lamp of our feet and the light of our path now and here. For all this common life of ours there are ideals that uplift and transfigure and ennoble it. There is an ideal for the home and for the church, for the school and for the shop, for the factory and for the city; and the one refreshing and inspiring experience of life is to get sight of it, and believe in it. The ideal in all these social organizations is nothing else but God's way,—the way that he has ordained for human beings to live and work together. The thing for us to do is first to discern it ourselves, and then to get men to see it, and believe in it, and work for it with heart and soul and mind and strength.[47]

Conclusions

It should be clear by now that Gladden's answer to the question as to whether the United States can be a Christian nation is affirmative, if it shows Christian behavior in its "purposes and policies and ruling aims."[48] Legislation and political office are avenues to accomplish this, but they are not the only ones, and invectives and unchristian political actions are not acceptable as means. It is not a question of trying to impose moral views on others, it is a question of advocating measures that can be demonstrated to be for the benefit of the common good, and attempting to convince majorities of the value of these measures. This is particularly important, and perhaps most challenging, in implementing programs to protect minorities, especially the poor, against the powerful.

A related question may be: Is the United States more or less Christian now than it was in Gladden's time? Clearly, the moral fiber of the nation has deteriorated, and this presents a significant challenge. There have been some positive developments in social programs. Social Security and Medicare can be recognized as Christian programs in their intent. The "charter" school movement may provide some opportunity for better education. These programs, immigration issues, and health care initiatives have been examples of bitter disputes, but controversy should not be a deterrent, but an invitation to be "civil" and open to dialog: "It would seem to be nearly inevitable that when government is of the people and by the people, and when the people are compassionate and kind, their compassion and kindness will find expression in their national life."[49]

Notes

1. Washington Gladden, *The Church and the Nation* (Springfield, Mass.: The Congregational Home Missionary Society, 1905), p. 4.
2. Ibid., p. 6.
3. Ibid., p. 4.
4. White, Ronald C. Jr. and C. Howard Hopkins, *Social Gospel: Religion and Reform in Changing America* (Philadelphia: Temple University Press, 1976), pp. 292-4.
5. Washington Gladden, *Recollections* (Boston: Houghton, Mifflin and Co., 1909), pp. 2-23, 33.
6. Ibid., p. 56.
7. I bid., p. 67.
8. Ibid., p. 89.
9. Handy, Robert T., *The Social Gospel in America* (New York: Oxford University Press, 1966), pp. 22-4.
10. Ibid., p. 23.
11. Dorn, Jacob Henry, *Washington Gladden* (Athens, Ohio: Ohio University Press, 1968), pp. 208-9.
12. Handy, Robert T., *The Social Gospel in America*, pp. 174-5.
13. Dorn, Jacob Henry, *Washington Gladden*, pp. 32-3.
14. Rauschenbusch, Walter, *Christianizing the Social Order* (New York: The Macmillan Co., 1926), p. 9.
15. Gladden, *Ruling Ideas of the Present Age* (Boston: Houghton, Mifflin and Co., 1895), p. 63.
16. Ibid., pp. 63-4.
17. Ely, Richard, *The Social Law of Service* (New York: Eaton and Maines, 1896), p. 127.
18. Cicero, *Three Books of Offices,* tr. Cyrus R. Edmonds (New York: Harper and Brothers, 1892), pp. 14-5.
19. Gladden, *The Christian Way* (New York: Dodd, Mead and Company, 1877), p. 104.
20. Gladden, *The Church and The Nation*, p. 6.
21. Gladden, *Commencement* Days (New York: The Macmillan Company, 1916), pp. 31-2.
22. Gladden, *The Church and The Nation*, p. 6.
23. Pope Leo XIII, *Rerum novarum [1891]* (The Vatican: Vatican Documents, 2010), p. 32.
24. Gladden, *Social Salvation* (Boston: Houghton, Mifflin and Company, 1902), p. 21.
25. Gladden, *The Christian Way* (New York: Dodd, Mead & Co., 1877), p. 115.
26. Ibid., p. 120.

27. Ibid., p. 115.
28. Gladden, *Social Salvation*, pp. 22-3.
29. Ely, Richard, *Ground Under Our Feet* (New York: The Macmillan Company, 1938), pp. 186-7.
30. Gladden, *Ruling Ideas of the Present Age*, pp. 95-6.
31. Pope Francis's Speech to the Congress of the United States, September 24, 2015.
32. Gladden, *The Church and Modern Life* (Boston: Houghton, Mifflin and Company, 1902), p. 154.
33. Ely, *The Social Law of Service* (New York: Eaton and Maines, 1896), pp. 172-3.
34. Rauschenbusch, *Christianity and the Social Crisis* (NY: The Macmillan Company: 1907), p. 373.
35. Gladden, *Things New and Old* (Columbus, Ohio: A.H. Smythe, 1883), p. 287.
36. Rauschenbusch, *Christianity and the Social Crisis*, p. 374.
37. Ely, Richard, *The Social Law of Service*, pp. 173-4.
38. Walzer, Michael, "The Concept of Civil Society," in Michael Walzer, ed., in *Toward a Global Civil Society* (New York: Berghahn Books, 2002), pp. 7-27, at 7.
39. Ibid., at 16.
40. Ibid., at 20.
41. Gladden, *The Church and the Nation*, p. 4.
42. Gladden, *Working People and their Employers* (New York: Funk and Wagnalls, 1888), p. 129.
43. Paul Ricoeur, *Interview with Hans Kung*, 1998.
44. Gladden, *Things New and Old*, p. 283.
45. Gladden, *The Church and the Kingdom* (New York: Fleming H. Revell Co., 1894), pp. 8, 11-2.
46. Rauschenbusch, *A Theology for the Social Gospel* (New York: The Macmillan Company, 1917), pp. 144-145.
47. Gladden, *Social Salvation*, pp. 28-9.
48. Gladden, *The Church and the Nation*, p 4.
49. Ibid., p. 7.

CROSSCURRENTS

RENOUNCING HARVARD: THE ASCETIC THEOLOGY OF JONATHAN TRAN

Thomas J. Millay

If the popularity of Sarah Coakley's recent books is any indication, ascetic theology is going through a period of rebirth.[1] Sources like Gregory of Nyssa and Augustine of Hippo are being newly plumbed for their ascetic wisdom, out of what seems a general sentiment that such wisdom has been lost and needs to be retrieved.[2] I believe that this renewal should be welcomed, yet also conceived more broadly than it has been up to the present moment.[3] In contemporary theological discourse, *askēsis* has been limited to topics having to do primarily with sexuality and concomitant disciplinings of the body. Such a restricted focus was not always the case. In fact, *askēsis* once described a whole field of renunciatory practices, only some of which were sexual in nature.

One way to recover this broader application of asceticism is to observe where renunciation shows up in contemporary theology and then highlight locales that are otherwise than sexual. An exemplary instance, notable for its avoidance of several pitfalls within ascetic theology, can be found in Jonathan Tran's essay "'The Spirit of God Was Hovering over the Waters': Pressing Past Racialization in the Decolonial Missionary Context; or, Why Asian American Christians Should Give Up Their Spots at Harvard."[4] In what follows, I first give a close reading to Tran's essay before suggesting how it can assist theologians attempting to expand the reach of a new asceticism. Key to this suggestion will be Tran's use of practical reason.

In the context of a book on missiology and whiteness, Tran's essay takes up a controversial topic: the recent lawsuit *Students For Fair Admissions v. Harvard* (filed in 2014), which alleges that Harvard has a policy of limiting Asian student enrollment and challenges the legality of such a policy. Through a series of complex negotiations with postracial ideology, Tran considers what a specifically Christian response to this situation should be. His essay unfolds in several steps.

After introducing the topic, Tran lays out the three theories of postracialism he sees as operative in contemporary discourse about race (231-234). In the first, called "simple postracialism," race was once a problem in North American society (that is, it was a source of discrimination), but it is so no longer. The election of Barack Obama is cited as proof of this fact. Next, "biological postracialism" posits a future in which the mixture of races generated by human reproductive activity will eventually make racism impossible. As Tran crassly if rather hilariously puts it, if everyone looks like Tiger Woods, racism not only won't but *can't* be a problem anymore. The last variety Tran describes is "aspirant postracialism," which holds that the best way to get past race is to stop using race as a categorical descriptor. In other words, we should act in accordance with the society want to have, rather than being overdetermined by our pasts. Aspirant postracialism believes that if we stop acting as if race is determinative, it will eventually stop being determinative. Chief Justice John Roberts, in his *Shelby County v. Holder* (2013) decision, is a prominent example of this way of thinking.

Tran then lays out the basics of the *SFFA v. Harvard* litigation, followed by the application and evaluation of the three postracial theories to this specific case (234-240). This section of the essay closes with a series of profound meditations on how, like Kant, postracialism relies on erasure of the past as an essential component of a more ethical future.

Affirmative action and decolonial theory, on the other hand, rely on thick conceptions of the past and its perdurance as a frame for ethical action in the present (240-242). Yet there is a danger here that needs to be addressed: if we are to use the past as a resource, how are we to do so without picturing that past as all-determinative, as a prison house that dictates every detail of our still racialized society? In order to articulate how receptivity to the past as a resource does not trap us in past horror, Tran turns to theological resources (242-245), and first of all to pneumatology. For Tran, the Holy Spirit stands for the possibility of a hope that does not rely on erasure of the past. By way of the Holy Spirit moving to introduce new life, past determination is not opposed to redemption, but is integrated into redemption's unfolding pattern. And what does this pattern look like, one might ask? This is an evangelical book, based on conversations held at Fuller Theological Seminary, so the answer is ready-at-hand: the unfolding pattern of redemption can be identified in lives that are growing daily in Christ-likeness.

Accepting that we will live in a racialized society for the foreseeable future, Tran then resources pneumatology and Christology to give a more specific answer to what it might look like 'to live missionally' (245) in such a society. His answer is specific to Asian Americans, and it develops as an exercise of practical reason in relation to the aforementioned *SFFA v. Harvard* case. Tran does decide on a course of action, and he proposes the following recommendation before delving into the logic that supports it:

> The Harvard case would be helped by one simple act: Asian American Christians admitted to Harvard going elsewhere, leaving available spots for non-Asian Americans, divesting themselves of the privileges and benefits that may have paved their way to places like Harvard. (246)

So, Tran's recommendation for Asian American Christians is simple refusal; though many Asian Americans are worthy of taking spots at Harvard, they should not consider such worth something to be grasped. Instead, they should renounce their admittance and leave the spots for others.

This refusal serves four primary goals: (1) it leaves open more spots at Harvard for those of less privileged background (this requires what Tran calls the recognition of 'if not White privilege, Yellow privilege' [248]); (2) it frees Asian American Christians from the trap of the model-minority myth; they are liberated from 'perform[ing] the script as it is written' (245); (3) it refuses to be lured into the warped terms set by American society, ruled as it is by White privilege, where minority groups are pitted against one another and left to fight over remaining scraps;[5] (4) it serves as a witness that there can be greater objectives for one's life than success such as it is defined by the world. For all these reasons, Tran argues that Asian American Christians should take his recommendation seriously, and it is difficult to argue against the fact that such refusal would be a profound, almost unimaginable act.

Let us take a moment to reflect on what is going on here, beyond the case-at-hand. To put it simply, Tran recommends renunciation. This places him within a broad legacy of Christian ascetic thought that recognizes the lure of the world and bids the faithful Christian to resist that lure through a variety of practices, such as fasting, continence, rough clothing, sleeplessness, and spiritual warfare—all of which can be placed within the general category of renunciation. Tran's recommendation may be different than these traditional examples, but it is recognizably a part of the same trajectory.

I will return in a moment to how Tran's theology is embedded within traditions of Christian asceticism. Before looking more deeply at the ascetic legacy at work in Tran's theology in a positive sense, I would like to point out that Tran deftly avoids two dangers endemic to the ascetic tradition.

(1) In Tran's theology, the ascetic practice of renunciation has a larger purpose: namely, *askēsis* is tied to the missional goal of witness. Too often, the ascetic tradition has fallen into recommending suffering for other reasons, such as avoiding pleasure, earning an eternal reward, or connecting more deeply to Christ.[6] All of these verge on elevating suffering into a kind of good, a potentially disastrous move with problems I return to below, in the form of a discussion of kenotic ethics.

Tying suffering to a larger purpose avoids the danger of valorizing suffering as a good in-itself. In Søren Kierkegaard's *Works of Love*, for example, the Christian is said to live in the category of the "double danger."[7] To live in the double danger is not only to renounce worldly glory, but also to receive upon oneself the hatred of the world precisely because of one's renunciation. For Kierkegaard, writing within the context of a comfortable-bourgeois Danish Christendom,[8] the embrace of suffering is a public act that results in anger being directed at the witnessing individual. Tran's call to renunciation forms a parallel: Asian American Christians are not to renounce Harvard simply for the sake of ruining their own lives. Instead, such renunciation should be a meaningful act of witness situated in such a way that it provokes a wider culture to puzzlement, at least, though possibly also rage.

(2) Tran's recommendation of renunciation is not universal. He does not believe every Asian American Christian student should renounce Harvard, let alone every student in general. Instead, renunciation is tied to an act of practical discernment: specifically, the recognition of one's own privilege. What follows is a restatement of Tran's recommendation, where he includes some crucial qualifications:

> Asian American Christians might look to participate in the Spirit's reparative missional work of God in Christ, the full and therefore vulnerable inhabitation of history that inscribes them in lives that might, as imagined through Philippians 2, recognize Asian American privilege where it obtains (it certainly does not always) and where it is recognized (it certainly is not always) and learn to, in good Philippian fashion, not consider privilege something to be held on to (246)

Again, Tran's recommendation of renunciation is not universal, and here he has provided a relevant criterion: privilege.[9] Whether or not Tran's asceticism applies to you thus depends on an act of discernment. One must sift through one's own life and see if this category of privilege applies to it. Only if the answer is 'yes' is renunciation an appropriate action; otherwise, its essential context is missing.

Tran's ascetic theology thus relies on an implied account of practical discernment. I take that account to be something like that offered by Oliver O'Donovan in his magisterial *Ethics as Theology* trilogy. O'Donovan calls practical discernment "practical reason," though I believe this to be potentially confusing considering the Kantian associations endemic to the phrase[10] (and O'Donovan is by no means a Kantian; in fact he eschews *a priori* reasoning at every turn). At any rate, O'Donovan's description of what he calls "practical reason" is helpful for thinking through the kind of reasoning Tran employs in proffering his ascetic recommendation:

> Practical reason is not deductive, but inductive.... Practical reason is not an inference from premises to conclusions. It has no premises, no points from which an uncontroversial start may be made, and it has no conclusions, on which its trains of reason come to rest. No premises, because the knowledge of the world on which practical reason turns is always contested, not agreed. No conclusions, because practical reason terminates in action, not in belief. The

> descriptive accounts of reality that afford an *entrée* for action are not agreed starting-points. They are complex readings of the world, and as such arguable from the beginning.[11]

O'Donovan develops this notion of practical reason's basis in "complex readings of the world" through his tripartite emphasis on personal experience,[12] the narratives which place that personal experience into an objective world,[13] and the communal wisdom and advice that enable one to coordinate personal experience with a story about the broader world in which one acts.[14] These three instantiations of practical reason result in awareness of the world in which one is acting and the place one holds in that world; this is what O'Donovan above calls "description."[15] In O'Donovan's scheme, then, ethical action rests on a host of contingent and particular factors. Little is gained through abstract principles, and much relies on the dense matrix of interdependent reasonings that lead up to an act.

Of course, O'Donovan is not alone in giving an account such as this; Stanley Cavell or Robert Brandom could also serve as resources for explicating Tran's reasoning.[16] Yet O'Donovan—by bringing together personal experience, narrative, and communal wisdom—usefully highlights the role discernment plays within ethics. And Tran's call to renunciation relies precisely on this factor of discernment. Based off one's own personal experience, the narrative of one's life and community, and the contextual advice given by one's community, one must decide whether or not the life one has lived can be categorized as privileged. If one accepts Tran's recommendation, one can then decide how to act. If one's life has been privileged, it is an act of Christian witness to renounce Harvard. If not, then not.

Incorporation of practical discernment with relation to an act that is not universally legislated helps to answer the strong objections that have been made with respect to the continuing viability of kenotic ethics (in regard to *kenosis*, see Tran's reference to Philippians 2, above). For example, Daphne Hampson calls such a renunciatory paradigm into question in her 1990 book *Theology and Feminism*:

> That [*kenosis*] should have featured prominently in Christian thought is perhaps an indication of the fact that men have understood what the male problem, in thinking in terms of hierarchy

and domination, has been. It may well be a model which men need to appropriate and which may helpfully be built into the male understanding of God. But ... *for women, the theme of self-emptying and self-abnegation is far from helpful as a paradigm.*[17]

According to Hampson, a universal call to *kenosis* serves to reinforce social inequality. It bids all to renounce without acknowledging the fact that some have more to renounce than others. This is why it is important that Tran builds subjective awareness of privilege into his account of renunciation; his recommendation is only applicable to those who would recognize themselves as privileged, as having something to renounce. Yet for those who do have something to renounce, and are able to recognize it, asceticism can be liberatory; it can result in what Tran labels "dispossessive empowerment" (249). Dispossession can be empowering because it can free a given subject from the constraints history, driven as it is by hegemonic forces, attempts to impose:

> Our dispossessive act, where and when it is possible, would reverse the lines of moral agency usually at play for ethnic minorities under strains of white supremacy, as evidenced by the lawsuit's [i.e., *SFFA v. Harvard*] wedging strategies. Instead, acting out of and toward mutuality, something always in need of attentive maintenance, such acts would avail and empower moral agency, a performative moment that explodes the model-minority myth (248-249).

Essentially, Hampson and Tran make the same point: renunciation, or a kenotic ethical imperative, is only appropriate in some situations, and which situations these might be requires the practice of what O'Donovan calls "description." Hampson and Tran are in agreement, only she focuses on a situation in which renunciation would be harmful, while he highlights a case in which renunciation would be empowering.

We have seen how Tran's ascetic theology avoids some of the pitfalls the ascetic tradition has fallen into in the past. But how is Tran's thought connected to that tradition? The example of Kierkegaard's asceticism-as-public witness has already been mentioned. There is one further historical resonance that can be added.

In the 14th-16th centuries, groups of devout Christians rejected promising clerical careers in order to dedicate themselves to lives of simplicity and moral witness. These groups, residing principally in the Dutch lowlands, are collectively known as the *devotio moderna* movement. According to John Van Engen, the elements common to the 'Devout experience' are as follows:

> conversion (teen or adult); breaking with family, with ecclesiastical promotion, with a career in learning; choosing to join a self-made urban commune sustained in part by manual labor; resolving to internalize and enact devotion in the face of suspicious townspeople and wary churchmen.[18]

To join the *devotio moderna* was to reject the script of success given to you. One's parents may have spent a considerable amount of money grooming one to be a member of the intellectual caste. Becoming a member of the Devout was thus a rejection of long-cherished expectations.[19] Instead of a comfortable, well-supported life of clerical labor,[20] one had to work with one's hands and live as part of a serious, penitential group of Christians whose official status in relation to the church was always precarious. In other words, the Devout had other goals in life than success.

Tran's call for privileged Asian American Christian students to renounce their Harvard acceptance thus has precedent in earlier forms of asceticism.[21] In fact, by connecting to these earlier forms, Tran pushes contemporary theology to recognize a wider scope for asceticism than is currently regnant.

If such a broader conception of asceticism is indeed unpopular in current theological writing (as I have noted), what is popular? Sarah Coakley's work is synonymous with a revival of asceticism in contemporary theological writing. She has written the eponymous book on the subject, titled *The New Asceticism*. With essays like "Beyond Libertinism and Repression: The Quest for a New Anglican Ascetics" and "Ecclesiastical Sex Scandals: The Lack of a Contemporary Theology of Desire," Coakley focuses insistently on issues of desire and sexuality. Building off material in the first volume of her systematic theology, *God, Sexuality, and the Self: An Essay 'On the Trinity'*, Coakley presents God as a kind of "third" who disrupts heteronormative desire between "the two."[22] Appropriation of such disruption is achieved through ascetic practices, particularly silence.[23] *Askēsis* enables access to divine desire, which destabilizes any and all human-to-human relations.

All of this certainly is certainly well-grounded in the ascetic traditions of Christian theology. Yet it also represents a certain narrowing of what asceticism can be. Coakley is surely right to affirm that human desire should not be reduced to sexuality.[24] However—at least so far in her work—she seems to performatively contradict this insight, in repeated returnings to issues of sexuality and gender. Given her context, narrowing asceticism to concerns with sexuality and gender can be understood as something strategic and laudable; Coakley consistently places her work within the context of a feminist theology also focused on sexuality and gender.[25] Yet—be that as it may—Coakley's own attention to her context or subject position should not abrogate the fact that ascetic theology is also able to speak about things such as the desire for success, and what it looks like to deny that desire, and—furthermore—how denial of that desire can be a Christian act of public witness.

All this leads back to Jonathan Tran and a final question about his work not sufficiently addressed thus far. Why call Tran's theology "ascetic," especially given the "negative associations of repression, ecclesiastical authoritarianism, and denial" often attached to asceticism?[26] Is such a label necessary? Perhaps it is not necessary, but it does good descriptive work. Tran's account of renunciation: (1) requires discipline, (2) rejects worldly success, (3) accepts the potential suffering that may result from the rejection of worldly success, and (4) is specifically patterned after the *kenosis* of Christ as described by Paul in Philippians 2. More important still than these multiple factors, (5) Tran's renunciatory recommendation bears public witness to Christian commitment, in a way similar to Kierkegaard's double danger. To call Jonathan Tran's theology 'ascetic', then, can tie all these characteristic factors together and give them concrete basis in a well-established mode of theology.

Ascetic theology may be well-established, but Tran shows how it can also breathe new life by continuing to issue productive solutions to theological or ideological dilemmas. Asceticism's potential ability to address issues of racial discrimination has yet to be tapped, which is why Tran's essay bears a certain amount of theoretical excitement for the reader while she is reading it. There is a further dimension to the work Tran is doing. Beyond issues of sexuality (where it is certainly also useful), Christian commitment to asceticism can fund acts of public witness that violate contemporary scripts of success. To be an ascetic is not to be repressed; it is to be liberated from the constraining claws of history.

From this last fact, we may conclude that the new asceticism should not only be expanded beyond the domain of sexuality; it should also not be separated from political theology. Jonathan Tran demonstrates that *askēsis* and Christian political witness can and sometimes should work in tandem. The precise conditions for advocating *askēsis* can never be completely established in advance, but as the new asceticism expands beyond sexuality, thinkers like Tran will become even more important as contemporary theologians perform the difficult work of discerning where the call to *askēsis* is appropriate and where inducement to renunciation is liberatory. Within an expanded new asceticism, the goal is dispossessive empowerment and the means is practical discernment. Guidance is needed.[27]

Notes

1. Interest in Coakley's work has generated an edited volume and numerous stand-alone articles. See McRandal, Janice, ed., *Sarah Coakley and the Future of Systematic Theology* (Minneapolis, MN: Fortress Press, 2016); Kirkland, Scott A., 2014, "Prayerful Dispossession and the Grammar of Thinking Theologically: Sarah Coakley and Gillian Rose," *New Blackfriars*, 95 (1060), November, pp. 662-73; Hilkert, Mary Catherine, 2014, "Desire, Gender, and God-Talk: Sarah Coakley's Feminist Contemplative Theology," *Modern Theology*, 30(4), October, 575-81; Green, Chris E.W., 2017, "Prayer as Trinitarian and Transformative Event in Sarah Coakley's *God, Sexuality, and the Self*," *Journal of Pentecostal Theology*, 26(1), March, 16-22.
2. On Gregory of Nyssa, see Smith, J. Warren, *Passion and Paradise: Human and Divine Emotion in the Thought of Gregory of Nyssa* (Chestnut Ridge, NY: Crossroad Publishing Company, 2004), Cadenhead, Raphael A., *The Body and Desire: Gregory of Nyssa's Ascetical Theology* (Oakland, CA: University of California Press, 2018). On Augustine of Hippo, see especially the work of Miles, Margaret R., *Desire and Delight: A New Reading of Augustine's "Confessions"* (Chestnut Ridge, NY: Crossroad Publishing Company, 1992), *Fullness of Life: Historical Foundations for a New Asceticism* (Philadelphia, PA: The Westminster Press, 1981). In addition, Peter Brown's *The Body and Society: Men, Women, and Sexual Renunciation in Early Christianity* (New York, NY: Columbia University Press, 1988) remains fundamental for contemporary attempts at retrieval.
3. As will become clear below, this is not so much a critique of Sarah Coakley as it is a recognition that she need not stand alone in the recovery of asceticism's potential.
4. See Sechrest, Love L., Johnny Ramírez-Johnson, and Amos Yong, eds., *Can "White" People Be Saved? Triangulating Race, Theology, and Mission* (Downers Grove, IL: InterVarsity Press, 2018), 229-52. Further references to this essay will be made in the text.
5. Ruether, Rosemary Radford makes a similar argument in *New Woman, New Earth* (New York, NY: Seabury Press, 1975), with respect to how white women should refuse to be positioned against black men.

6. Cohen's, Esther, *The Modulated Scream: Pain in Late Medieval Culture* (Chicago, IL: The University of Chicago Press, 2010) is an excellent resource on this topic.

7. See Millay, Thomas J., 'Kierkegaard, Imitation and Contemporaneity: The Importance of the Double Danger', *The Heythrop Journal*, forthcoming.

8. On this context, see especially Kirmmse, Bruce H., *Kierkegaard in Golden Age Denmark* (Bloomington, IN: Indiana University Press, 1990). Here as elsewhere in the present essay, my references to context can be only schematic in nature. My focus is on the formal category of thought (i.e., practical discernment) that is necessary for a contemporary revival of asceticism; thus I cannot do full justice to the various social contexts I evoke, which each deserve their own extended exegesis. See also below, n. 29.

9. For contemporary scholarly literature on privilege, see the useful review by Akin Taiwo in his dissertation 'The Praxis of Privilege: How Social Workers Experience Their Privilege' (University of Windsor, 2018), 17–43.

10. O'Donovan is, of course, aware of this. He makes useful distinctions between his position and both Kant and Aquinas in *Self, World, and Time: Ethics as Theology, Volume 1* (Grand Rapids, MI: William B. Eerdmans Publishing Company, 2013), 29–30.

11. *Self, World, and Time*, 30.

12. See *Self, World, and Time*, 11–14.

13. Being influenced by Paul Ricœur's account of narrative's ability to relate the subjective to the objective (see Ricœur's *Time and Narrative* trilogy [Chicago: University of Chicago Press, 1984–1988], and Millay, Thomas J., 'In this Second Case, History: Fredric Jameson's Reading of Paul Ricœur's *Temps et récit*', *Telos: Critical Theory of the Contemporary*, Spring 2016, 75-91), I take this to be a fair summary of O'Donovan's argument as developed in *Self, World, and Time*, 10–11 (and see his own endorsement of the word in *Self, World, and Time*, 3). However, O'Donovan himself generally shies away from the word because of its use by narrative ethicists (see *Self, World, and Time*, 36-8, for a critique of narrative ethics).

14. See *Self, World, and Time*, 12: 'Precisely because we know the world is objective, we know that the processing of experience by community criticism and tradition is needed'; cf. 60-61, 49-52, on wisdom and advice (respectively).

15. On description, see further especially *Self, World, and Time*, 11.

16. See Cavell, Stanley, *The Claim of Reason* (Oxford: Oxford University Press, 1979); Brandom, Robert, *Making It Explicit* (Cambridge, MA: Harvard University Press, 1994).

17. Hampson, Daphne, *Theology and Feminism* (Oxford: Basil Blackwell, 1990), 155.

18. Van Engen, John, *Sisters and Brothers of the Common Life: The Devotio Moderna and the World of the Later Middle Ages* (Philadelphia, PA: University of Pennsylvania Press, 2008), 2.

19. See Engen, Van, *Sisters and Brothers of the Common Life*, 139: "upon finishing Latin school... They then faced options: going to university (if they had money), seeking a position in church or court or town (if they had connections), prowling for a job requiring 'clerical' skills, seeking entrance to a religious order. Beginning around 1400, another option was to join a Brothers' household, free of vows, freed of seeking a job in the world, settled in a quiet spiritual community. Nearly no men, in striking contrast with the women, get described as entering out of social necessity or awkward circumstances, though plainly student-clerics with poor prospects may have fit that description. Choosing this form of life took a certain resolve, because its status was widely adjudged humiliating, if not downright

strange or suspicious, especially compared to what clerics would ordinarily hope or aim for. They even had to engage in manual labor, not the mark of 'bookmen'."

20. To be a "cleric" in this context was to be a lawyer who dealt specifically with ecclesiastical legal decisions. See Van Engen, *Sisters and Brothers of the Common Life*, 138, 151.

21. On the *devotio moderna* as an ascetic movement (rather than a mystical one), see especially Van Engen, *Sisters and Brothers of the Common Life*, 79.

22. See Coakley, Sarah, *God, Sexuality, and the Self: An Essay 'On the Trinity'* (Cambridge: Cambridge University Press, 2013), especially 24 and 56-8; *The New Asceticism: Sexuality, Gender and the Quest for God* (London: Bloomsbury, 2015), 96-100.

23. Coakley, *God, Sexuality, and the Self*, 340-4; *The New Asceticism*, 85.

24. Coakley, *God, Sexuality, and the Self*, 7-11; *The New Asceticism*, 6-10.

25. See especially the Preface to Coakely, *Powers and Submissions: Spirituality, Philosophy and Gender* (Oxford: Blackwell Publishing, 2002), xii-xx.

26. Coakley, *The New Asceticism*, 4.

27. I have not paid attention to my own context in this essay, which is that of a male within White American Christianity. Such work is undoubtedly required. As Metzel, Johnathan M. and Angela Denker's recent books *Dying of Whiteness* (New York, NY: Hachette Book Group, 2019) and *Red State Christians* (Minneapolis, MN: Fortress Press, 2019) make clear, there is a difference between lack of privilege and loss of privilege, with the latter carrying its own particular pathos. The difficult task of addressing my own context must include elements of ascetic wisdom that make sense of why one would want to renounce a politics of resentment that attempts to reassert authority, while at the same time recognizing the real exploitation of rural white America, with its connections to the ravages of globalized capitalism, extractive industries, and the engineering of the opioid crisis, which together qualify a univocal notion of 'privilege' in its application to White American Christians. As one can see from the broad territory just staked out, properly addressing this context requires (at least) a full-length essay dedicated to the topic. What I have instead aimed to do in this essay is—with Jonathan Tran as a guide—to practice the type of thinking that is necessary to undertake this separate and demanding task.

CROSSCURRENTS

MENTAL ILLNESS, THE SECOND AMENDMENT AND GUN VIOLENCE

Eugene P. Trager

The second amendment states that "A Well Regulated Militia, being necessary to the security of a free state, the right of the people to keep and bear Arms, shall not be infringed.[1] But what does this awkwardly worded statement really mean? Many Americans think it means that except for criminals and the mentally ill, we the people, have a constitutional right to own a firearm be it a handgun, a semi-automatic rifle or an AK 47. For many Americans, the 2nd amendment right to own a gun has the same hallowed status as the other nine amendments enshrined in the Bill of rights of the Constitution of the United States in 1791, including the right to free speech, to freedom of the press, to freedom of assembly, to be protected from unreasonable search and seizure, the right not to be deprived of life, liberty or property without due process, the right to a speedy public trial by an impartial jury of one's peers and the right to be protected from cruel and unusual punishment. If there is to be a fruitful dialogue between Gun Rights advocates and Gun Control advocates, both groups must appreciate, empathize and respect the powerful emotions on both sides of the gun divide.

Many people feel that gun violence is primarily due to criminals and the mentally ill and that if we had stricter criminal laws, longer sentences, stricter mental health regulations, better treatments for the mentally ill and more counselling for troubled people, we could reduce gun violence in the United States. This is true to an extent, but there is more to it than that. Our nation's gun violence is a public health epidemic. All nations in the world including advanced industrial countries have similar rates of mental illness and emotionally troubled people, yet they vastly differ in the number of shootings compared to the United States. According to the massive database maintained by the University of Washington which tracks lives lost in every country, in every year by every possible cause of death, gun deaths in the United States is 27 times higher than Denmark and, excluding terrorism, at least 10 times higher than Britain, Germany, Canada and Japan. Mental Illness and troubled people are everywhere—Gun violence is not!

Only a small percentage of mentally ill people are more prone to violent acts than the general population. The majority of violent acts, by sheer number are committed by people who would not meet psychiatric criteria for mental illness and a significant number have no previous criminal record. Instinctively, people think that most violent criminal acts must be a product of mental illness, but criminality is not tantamount to mental illness. Politicians have avoided taking positions on gun control reform by using an expanded category of mental illness in which troubled people are included, as a convenient and politically safe explanation for gun violence. While there may be troubled, unhappy, frustrated and angry people in the United States because of their socio-economic and domestic circumstances, and such people may be more prone to gun violence, to label these people mentally ill is a self-serving metaphorical stretch. Problems in living are not mental illness.

One of the few legally enforceable restrictions on *individual* gun ownership in every state involves diagnosed mental patients involuntarily hospitalized for potentially violent behavior where access to guns is assessed and suitable restrictions on gun ownership are imposed. Where there is reasonable concern about risk of violence in a person with mental illness, laws in virtually every state mandate that mental health professionals take responsibility to competently and thoroughly assess that risk and make clinical and legal recommendations about how best to deal with it, including hospitalizing the patient, warning potential victims and taking the patient's guns away. This requirement is memorialized as "The Tarasoff Principle"[2] based on a case that was adjudicated by the California Supreme Court and is known as the duty to protect.

Could mental health laws be stricter in terms of criteria for involuntary hospitalization and involuntary assessment and treatment of potential dangerous mental patients on an outpatient basis. Yes. But then how do we contend with conflicting constitutional concerns about liberty and privacy. Where do we draw the line?

In focusing on the Second Amendment, this article will attempt to show whether and to what extent there is a connection between the second amendment and gun violence in the United States. The history of second amendment begins with an obvious question. Why was it adopted? In 1791, the states threatened to refuse to ratify the Constitution of the United States if their right to keep their state militias was infringed. There was concern that the Federalists would allow the national government to dismantle or disarm the state militias. The purpose of the second amendment was to address those concerns and prevent that from happening. That was precisely why James Madison drafted the second amendment and that is why the second amendment begins with the statement, "A well-regulated militia being necessary to the security of a free state..."

At the time of the adoption of the Second Amendment, continuing in the 19th century and up to and including the present, states could and did regulate *individual* ownership of various kinds of guns. Adam Winkler, professor of Constitutional law at the University of California and a respected constitutional scholar, gives many such examples of states over the years, regulating and restricting individual gun ownership including an Alabama court ruling that it was a state's right to regulate where and how a citizen could carry a gun, Louisiana upholding its ban on concealed carry of a gun and Kentucky adopting an amendment to its Constitution to specify that the state was within its rights to regulate or prohibit concealed carry of guns.[3]

While prior to the 2008 Supreme Court decision, the 2nd amendment did not confer a federal constitutional right for an individual to own and keep guns, forty-three state constitutions did protect the right of an individual to own and keep guns, many of these provisions dating back to the nation's founding. However, it was understood that this right was subject to state regulation and as indicated above, states did pass laws regulating individual gun ownership.[4]

Although the framers of the second amendment were not concerned with establishing a federal constitutional right for *individuals* outside of a militia to own and keep guns, people during the revolutionary period certainly were concerned about an individual constitutional right to own guns, which is why most state constitutions protected that right. Where did this idea about a constitutional right of individuals to own guns come from? It came from The English Declaration of Rights of 1689 which stated, "Whereas King James the Second, by the assistance of [many] evil counsellors, judges and ministers employed by him, did endeavor to subvert and extirpate the Protestant religion and the laws and liberties of this kingdom, all Protestants have the right to bear arms for their defense, suitable to their conditions and as allowed by law." But did the English Declaration of Rights actually give individuals the right to own and use guns? According to Lois Schwoerer, Professor of History and author of the book, *The Declaration of Rights, 1689*,[5] The English Declaration of 1689 did not give individuals the right to own and use guns and did not say that the government couldn't restrict individual gun ownership (everyone accepted that it could and did), but rather who could do so, King or Parliament. Parliament passed laws and the King was obliged to respect Parliament's law-making authority. The Declaration of 1689 stated that the Catholic King James II of England was attempting to "subvert and extirpate the Protestant religion and the laws of the Kingdom" by disbanding Protestant militias, taking guns away from Protestants and re-establishing Catholic rule as it was in England prior to Henry VIII. This was considered an Insurrection! The purpose of the English Declaration was to suppress that insurrection by providing guns to upper class, land-owning Protestants— not to establish the legal right of individuals, to own guns. In fact, members of the lower socio-economic classes were prohibited from owning most kinds of guns. None the less, American Gun advocates, influenced by the English Declaration of 1689, were determined to try to use the second amendment as a vehicle to establish a constitutional right for individuals to own and use guns, even though that was not the purpose of the second amendment.

It should be noted that the phrase "suitable to their conditions and as allowed by laws" in the English Declaration of Rights, referred to laws already on the books that limited gun ownership to upper-class Englishmen, so that in effect, only a relatively small minority of Englishmen had a legal right to own guns reflecting the fear of arming the lower classes by a hierarchical British society.

For over 200 years after the adoption of the Second Amendment, it was uniformly understood that the second amendment did not say that an individual, who was not a member of the militia had a constitutional right to keep and bear arms. No court had ever found that an individual had a federal constitutional right to own a gun. In fact the Supreme court ruled three times on this issue, in 1876,[6] 1886,[7] and 1939 [8]and on each occasion held that it granted the people a right to bear arms only within a militia as defined in Article 1, section 8 of the Constitution of the United States.

All that changed in 2008 when the Supreme Court of the United States, led by Justice Antonin Scalia in Columbia v. Heller, held that the Second Amendment does protect an individual's right to possess a firearm, and disconnected this right with service in a militia. This was the first Supreme Court case in history to decide that the Second Amendment protects an *individual's* right to own a gun. But did the Supreme Court in 2008 re-interpret the second amendment or did it simply validate America's gun affirming culture?

The Holding of Columbia v. Heller was that, "The Second Amendment guarantees an individual's constitutional right to possess a firearm unconnected with service in a militia, and to use that arm for lawful purposes." The case was decided by a 5 to 4 vote. Voting in the majority lead by Scalia, were Roberts, Kennedy, Thomas and Alito. Voting in the Dissent were Breyer, Souter, Ginsberg and Stevens.

In order to get Justice Kennedy's crucial swing vote, Scalia agreed to include the statement that guns and gun ownership could still continue to be regulated. When asked, "who will do the regulating, Scalia answered, "the culture will determine how guns will be regulated in the future." In fact, given this "new interpretation" of the second amendment, the right of the culture to regulate gun ownership in the future will probably be curtailed.

This was born out when in February of 2019, the Bipartisan Background Checks Act of 2019, a bill that would require Federal background check for every firearm purchase, was approved by the U.S. House of Representatives. According to several independent polls done in the last two years, between 75-80% of Americans support uniform Federal background checks in every state for every gun purchase as well as other gun control laws and consider them to be reasonable.[9]

Gun advocates objected to the bill, fearing that such universal background checks will go beyond determining if people have a documented criminal or mental illness record, in order to take their guns away, but will target troubled people like gun-owning stalkers, jilted boyfriends and angry grudge holders who are thought to be at risk for gun violence (red flag laws) so that their guns can legally be removed. Trump advocates immediately stated that such a bill would be vetoed because it violates the constitutional right of an individual who is not charged as a criminal or certified as mentally ill, to own guns. Will the recent mass shootings in El Paso and Dayton change Trump's mind? Will conservative Supreme Court Justices like Gorsuch and Kavanaugh be less likely to use the second amendment as a justification for declaring unconstitutional gun control laws the culture considers to be reasonable?

Gun advocates often point out that the Second Amendment says the right of "the people" to keep and bear arms shall not be infringed? Doesn't this mean that an individual has a constitutional right to own and use guns. If the second amendment was referring only to the right of militia members to own guns, why didn't it just say, the right of state militias to keep and bear arms shall not be infringed?

According to Scalia "the people" literally meant individuals. That was his understanding based on his "originalism" doctrine which purports to determine what the original meaning of the second amendment was and states that the Constitution should be interpreted "as written." However, while the Harvard Law review points out that in the 4th amendment, the right of "the people" to be protected against unreasonable searches and seizures, clearly refers to individuals,[10] in the 2nd amendment "the people" clearly refers to the group of people who were members of a militia according to Paul Finkelman.[11] Finkelman also pointed out that James Madison. who drafted the 2nd amendment, was clearly referring to a "body of the people" who were members of a militia.

Consider Madison's first draft of the proposed 2nd amendment as modified by the committee of the House to which Madison's draft was referred: "A well-regulated militia composed of *the body* of the people, being the best security of a free state, the right of the people to keep and bear arms shall not be infringed, but no person religiously scrupulous shall be compelled to bear arms." This suggests two points. The first point is that the framers clearly saw this draft as an amendment about the militia, a military body: that any right to own weapons was a right of militia members as a collective body, derived from the right of each state to maintain a "well-regulated militia."

The second point referred to an exemption for pacifists or conscientious objectors. This suggests that the militias were composed of volunteers as well as draftees and the issue that concerned the framers of the second amendment, was whether pacifists should be exempt from military service in the militia not whether individuals had a constitutional right to bear arms. Furthermore, at the time of the writing of the second amendment, the term "bear arms" clearly referred to military service. Although gun advocates like to equate "bearing arms" with carrying a gun, to James Madison the term, "to bear arms" meant to render military service in a state militia or a national army.[12]

According to Gary Wills, noted Constitutional scholar and Professor at Northwestern University, Evanston, Illinois, the phrase, "keep and bear arms" in the second amendment was always used in a military context. You wouldn't say people had a right to keep and bear arms to protect themselves or to hunt rabbits or deer. You would say people had a right to own a pistol, shotgun or a rifle to protect themselves, and to hunt rabbits or deer. If the framers of the second amendment had intended to protect the individual right to own a gun, why didn't they simply say, "Congress shall have no power to prohibit private ownership of guns?"[13]

So how did Scalia, a brilliant constitutional scholar, who prides himself on interpreting the law as written and who railed against justices he accuses of legislating from the bench, explain his position that the second amendment gives individuals who are not Militia members, a constitutional right to own and keep guns in the face of three Supreme Court findings that the second amendment conferred a right to bear arms only within a militia?

Scalia's explanation was that he divided the second amendment into a prefatory clause ("well-regulated militia") and an operative clause ("right of the people to keep and bear arms"). Then, based on some laws with prefatory and operative clauses in which he claimed the prefatory clause did not limit the operative clause, he arbitrarily decided that the "militia" in the prefatory language expressed the 2nd amendment's purpose, but it did not limit the scope of the operative clause, "right of the people to keep and bear arms," which could be expanded to include an individual not in the militia who would have a constitutional right to own a gun.

In addressing Scalia's explanation, William G. Merkel, a Constitutional Scholar, in a symposium on the second amendment commented that "Justice Scalia operates with the faith-based assumption that the framers must have intended to protect a private right to gun possession and then manipulated outlying evidence to dress up his claim in ill-fitting pseudo-academic garb. In the process he demonstrated conclusively that the originalist methodology he trumpeted in *A Matter of Interpretation* as the surest remedy against judicial injection of subjective values into constitutional adjudication was in fact nothing more than a hollow sham."[14] In other words, in District of Columbia v. Heller, Scalia was simply validating our gun affirming culture, a culture he identified with long before the District of Columbia v. Heller Supreme Court decision. While there is nothing inherently wrong with a gun affirming culture, the question remains, can you have a gun affirming culture without gun violence?

So, what does the second amendment have to do with gun violence? Actually, very little. As long as there are more guns in this country than there are people, as long as there are people who love guns and fear that the government wants to take away their guns, as long as people feel they need guns for their protection and resent gun regulation, gun violence will continue regardless of how the second amendment is interpreted or even if it is repealed as the late Justice John Paul Stevens suggested. Will future generations have the temerity to outlaw assault weapons, buy back those in circulation, and require individuals to qualify for a license to own a gun like we do to own a car, since both can be deadly weapons? Australia, New Zealand, England and other gun-owning, freedom-loving democratic countries did that. It drastically reduced gun violence in those countries. It could do the same in the United States.

Notes

1. The Constitution of the United States, Amendment II (1791) But
2. Tarasoff v. Regents of the University of California, 17 Cal. 3d 425, 551 P.2d 334, 131 Cal.Rptr. 14 (Cal 1976)
3. Winkler, Adam, *Gunfight: The Battle Over the Right to Bear Arms in America* (New York: W.W. Norton and Company, Inc., 2011), p. 166.
4. Ibid, p. 33.

5. Schwoerer, Lois, "To Hold and Bear Arms: The English Perspective," in *The Second Amendment in Law and History* (New York: The New Press, 2002), pp. 211-7.
6. U.S. v. Cruikshank, 92 U.S. 542 (1876)
7. Presser v. Illinois, 116 U.S. 252 (1886)
8. U.S. v. Miller, 307 U.S. 174 (1939)

The Miller Court wrote: The Constitution as originally adopted granted to Congress power "To provide for calling forth the Militia to execute the Laws of the Union, suppress insurrections and repel invasions; To provide for organizing, arming and disciplining, the Militia, and for governing such Part of them as may be employed in the service of the United States, reserving to the States respectively, The appointment of Officers, and the Authority of training the Militia according to the discipline prescribed by Congress." U.S.C.A. Const, art 1,8. With obvious purpose to assure the continuation and render possible the effectiveness of such forces the declaration and guarantee of the Second Amendment were made. It must be interpreted and applied with that end in view.

U.S v. Miller, *supra* note 4, at 178.
9. The Economist (Print Edition United States, Los Angeles), *What Works to Reduce Gun Deaths*, March 22, 2018.
10. *Harvard Law Review*, 126, pp. 1079-80.
11. Finkelman, Paul, "A Well-Regulated Militia: The Second Amendment in Historical Perspective," in *The Second Amendment in Law and History* (New York: The New Press, 2002), p. 139.
12. Heyman, Steven J., "Natural Rights and the Second Amendment," in *The Second Amendment in Law and History* (New York: The New Press, 2002), p. 202.
13. Wills, Garry, *A Necessary Evil: A History of American Distrust of Government* (New York: First Touchtone Edition, 2002), pp. 191-260.
14. Merkel, William G., "The Second Amendment in Context: The Case of the Vanishing Predicate," *Chicago Kent Law Review* 76(1), pp. 403-4.

BOOK REVIEW

THE PURITANS: A TRANSATLANTIC HISTORY

The Puritans: A Transatlantic History. By David Hall. Princeton Univ. Press, Princeton, NJ 2019. 517 pp. $35.

The troubles with this fiercely learned and astonishingly detailed book might be said to begin with its jacket. Note that Hall, a professor emeritus of American Religious history at Harvard Divinity School, is *not* covering the whole gigantic polymorphous phenomenon labeled with the usually pejorative, if not sneering, term "Puritanism." He is addressing the theological and political vicissitudes of a Reform movement in England, Scotland, and last of all America, from roughly the latter part of the reign of Henry VIII (d. 1547) to 1662, shortly after the Restoration of James II, when the Church of England ejected some 1,600 non-conforming ministers, who would forever afterwards be known as the Dissenters. This is still a vast stretch of territory; and one can think of all sorts of world-historical figures, who might have graced Hall's cover: Calvin? Cromwell? Milton? Instead we get only a clipped-in-half reproduction showing the lower half of the nose, the wispy van dyke mustache, and mouth of one Edward Winslow.

Who was Edward Winslow (1595–1655), you ask? Well, he was a Separatist (from the C. of E.) and at one time governor of Plymouth colony, who later created a small stir by defending the work of John Eliot's evangelizing among the Algonquian Indians. Hall tells us next to nothing about him otherwise; and so he becomes just another officer in the vast army of preaching, pamphleteering, hyperactive, but generally colorless and faceless divines we meet here who laid the foundations and built the formidable intellectual structures of Puritanism. This isn't, strictly speaking, Hall's fault. He doesn't have the time or space to fill out a three-dimensional social and cultural picture of his subject. (And there already is a formidable literature on that subject, e.g., in the *Cambridge Companion to Puritanism,* 2008). What he aims at and succeeds in presenting, though in a narrative devoid of vivid scenes, is a vigorous defense of Puritanism as a noble body of thought, as opposed to some sort of mass neurosis.

Though fair-minded and objective, there's no doubt how warmly Hall feels about a group of Christians whose language he often borrows in straightforwardly referring to them as "the godly." The passion infusing this apologia seems to be fueled by two obvious negative facts: (1) the Puritans have, from the earliest days, been doused with withering caricatures that have long outlasted their original targets. We remember Ben Jonson's Tribulation Wholesome and Zeal-of-the-Land Busy (from *The Alchemist*) and, before that, Sir Toby Belch's famous harpooning of Malvolio in *Twelfth Night* ("Dost thou think, because thou art virtuous, there shall be no more cakes and ale?") Later characters like Hawthorne's Roger Chillingworth of Dickens' Scrooge offer ammunition for H.L. Mencken's immortal definition of Puritanism as the "haunting fear that someone, somewhere may be happy." (2) The second motive behind Hall's argument is the dissolution, beginning in the eighteenth century, of the in-depth, philosophically serious (though admittedly severe) Puritan teachings and their replacement by more or less Arminian popular evangelism ("preparation for salvation") or merely humanistic Unitarianism, both of which Hall firmly disavows. The great documents of Puritanism, like The Westminster Confession of Faith (1646) are now by and large a dead letter, as are Calvinism and classic Presbyterianism. And so a great tradition has been dissipated.

However one feels about this, and however reasonably one may accuse Hall of underestimating some of the aesthetic deficits of Puritanism (what, endless psalm-singing, and no *Missa Papae Marcelli* or *Spem in alium*? No Bach chorales or Handel oratorios? No spectacular Baroque and Rococo churches? None of the treasures of sacred art from Giotto to Michelangelo to El Greco and beyond?) Hall certainly provides an exhaustive, coherent exposition of what Puritanism, in its prime, was all about. It meant, in no specific order, a grand ensemble of themes, including

1. The rejection of "idolatry," which spanned a vast spectrum of mainly Catholic practices and rituals (condemning even apparently trivial customs like wearing a surplice) and all sorts of behavior from venerating sacred images to pub-crawling;

2. A keen sense of the omnipresence of sin (thanks, Augustine!), the corruptibility and decadence of human nature, and the permanent dangers they posed to the church and society;

3. The belief that God's law bound civil society as well as the church, and so there could be no Jeffersonian wall separating church and state. (No surprise there, since Jefferson's shortened New Testament, "The Life and Morals of Jesus of Nazareth," completely excluded the supernatural);

4. Adding "the judicial laws of Moses," e.g., with reference to the Sabbath and the condemnation of adultery, to British law. By contrast, all the old feast days (no more pagan-flavored Christmas!), saints' days, and other church festivities had to go (and again Hall underestimates the cultural loss this might amount to);

5. Demanding that both civil governments and monarchs uphold "wholesome Lawes" of all sorts and publicly rebuking offenders against them. (But Puritans could never unanimously agree on the precise limits of royal authority);

6. Reliance on a "Word-based" rather than sacramental ministry to transform the faithful. This could be cynically dismissed as no more than a lot of long sermons; but the Reformers were keenly aware of how ill-trained many Catholic priests had been and thus incapable of actually proclaiming the message of the Gospel;

7. Stressing repentance and subsequent "sanctification." The consciousness that one was "walking uprightly before the Lord" provided assurance of personal salvation for those wrestling with the often traumatic issue of predestination;

8. Insisting on discipline as a mark of the true church, which meant elders keeping a sharp eye on the actual behavior of local parishioners, and in many cases waging war on the "unbridled license of ungodly living;"

9. Restricting access to baptism and Holy Communion to those judged worthy of grasping their significance and living in accordance with their prerequisites;

10. A vision of the unique relationship uniting "the godly" in their identity as the Body of Christ. One English minister described the ideal Christian community as follows: "There is, or can be, the like love to another, the like care for one another; the like spiritual watchfulness one over another; the like union and communion of members in one mystical body, in a sympathy of affections ..." (What non-Puritan believer could quarrel with that?)

11. Linking "a reformation of manners to the workings of divine providence," aka Providentialism, or reading individual and communal experiences (both blessings and tribulations) as divine judgments. Obviously, this approach was not limited to the Puritans and could prompt all sorts of quirky subjective responses to daily events;

12. Encouraging literacy among lay people, so as to advance the knowledge of Scripture and divine law: a movement that also had enormous, long-term non-religious consequences;

13. Regarding social injustice and pauperization as sinful and attempting to undo them (a colossal and highly laudable endeavor, to be sure);

14. In a similar vein, equating "equity" and "justice" as righteousness, and hence calling for changes in civil and criminal law;

15. Accepting the power of the civil state and the church to coerce as a necessary part of comprehensive reform, even while hoping for voluntary participation in such domination;

16. Calling for control of "appetites for worldly goods." This led to the condemnation to popular customs such as card-playing and dancing. Female sexuality and clothing came, as is well known, under particular scrutiny here (but one could find the same bias far back as the third chapter of 1 Peter);

Hall treads lightly when it comes to aspects of Puritanism that have been scathingly criticized for ages. He praises Calvin, but never mentions his burning of Michael Servetus at the stake. He writes edifying pages about John Knox but says nothing about his most notorious work, *The First Blast Against the Monstrous Regiment of Women* (1558). He doesn't consider that phenomena like the War on Drugs might be considered belated (and worse than futile) after-effects of Puritanism. He is painfully sensitive about the Enlightenment's success in tarring and feathering Puritanism in the secular mind, and so is wholly intent on righting the balance.

St. Paul in 1 Cor. 5 and elsewhere bade his followers expel from the Christian community and shun openly immoral believers, and the Puritans often tried to do the same. Thanks to original sin and human nature, establishing an ideal, "purified" body of worshipers, in some ways akin to a monastery, was bound to fall short (as if anticipating Nietzsche's acidulous remark that he might have believed in the Redeemer if his followers *looked* more redeemed (*Thus Spoke Zarathustra*, Part II, "The Priests").

Another insoluble problem—and something the conservative Hall doesn't go near—is the very nature of the first Christian community. Most scholarly commentators agree that Matthew's foundational logion in 16.18, "You are Peter and on this rock I will build my church" is a later addition, like making the Holy Spirit part of the Trinity (in Mt. 28.19). To put it bluntly, there is no specific evidence that Jesus ever intended to found the kind of institution we call a church; and the often bitter arguments between Paul and his ideological adversaries about the nature of the Church in Acts and the Letters show fluid and contested the structure of the Church was in the first century. The Puritan insistence on *sola Scriptura* didn't have enough information to work with.

So, Puritan theologians hunting for eternally valid proof texts to justify their own denominational alterations of Catholicism were in some ways on a wild goose chase. They were right to maintain that the modest New Testament Greek word later translated as bishop, *episkopos* (=overseer), had little in common with the remit of the powerful ecclesiastical lords of the Catholic Middle Ages; but expanding a few verses in 1 Cor.13, for example, about the various roles of ministers in the primitive Church into a sort of timeless Platonic blueprint of the perfect Jesus-based community was impossible. And even if the ecclesial arrangements found in Scripture had presented a clear cut, wholly coherent picture, where did the sixteenth- and seventeenth-century Puritan "originalists" derive their certainly that there was no room for evolution or alteration in the Christian modes of self-government during the ages to come? The Church fathers had little trouble in eliminating the active role of female "ministers" mentioned in some of Paul's letters and "the apostle Junia" in Rom. 16.7 (though, of course he condemned women to silence in church assemblies; see 1 Cor. 14.34).

One of the most interesting, if ultimately incalculable, aspects of Hall's history is the contribution made by the Puritans to both civil and churchly democracy. In their rage against "priestcraft," their demolition of the lofty pyramid of clerical offices, their championing of the individual conscience, and openness to liberated reading of Scripture, in fashions sometimes plain and direct and sometimes wildly idiosyncratic (denouncing the papacy as the Whore of Babylon and the pope as the Anti-Christ, or the sign of the cross or kneeling to receive the Eucharist as abominations), Puritans were carrying out a "leveling" operation. But they were not necessarily champions of human rights: many of them heartily supported trials for witchcraft and savagely attacked Quakers. Still, they undoubtedly gave individuals (i.e., men) a larger role to play in church administration and activities than the Catholic Church, which remains a monarchy to this date.

The Puritans is a formidable achievement; but its greatest strength has a dark shadow. Hall cites many scores of now forgotten (except by academic historians) theological writers and their vast outpouring of treatises and controversial writings; but he never suggests that they may have earned their oblivion. Particularly when it comes to the doctrine of double predestination, he doesn't seem to acknowledge its inhuman irrationality and how frequently traumatic its impact could be. In fact, he mourns the loss of the Puritan ideal of a "church composed of the worthy few." Predestination did have a scriptural foundation of sorts: Matthew 7. 14: "Strait is the gate, and narrow the way, which leadeth unto life, and few there be that find it." And Paul wrote in Romans 8.28-29 that "for whom (i.e., those who love God), he did foreknow, he also did predestinate to be conformed to the things of his Son"). But that did nothing to explain the part played by free will in becoming one of the chosen, apart from the "many" who were "called."

And, crucially because "the law" convicted the soul of sin without erasing the guilt incurred, there was no way to be confident of salvation except —though only imperfectly—by the evidence of a virtuous life. Good works in themselves were no guarantee of anything. Unmerited grace was everything; You could not earn entrance to heaven. Again, Hall won't concede the possibility that this dogma might be flawed, that, despite the anathemas heaped on his head, Pelagius night have been right in his assessment of the intrinsic power of human goodness, and that Augustine's view of original sin might have been intolerably harsh. Puritans preached about divine love a lot more than is usually recognized, but there is no discounting their emphasis on what Paul in Philippians 2.12 famously called "fear and trembling." Hall admits that, "The ministers and poplar writers who brandished the weapon of terror took for granted the merits of doing so."

The mass of English, Scottish, and American Puritans Hall quotes knew exactly what they wanted, a church composed of "visible Saints." They thought that however difficult, the ideal wasn't hopelessly utopian. The institutional framework they build for it has broken down; but who knows, perhaps they succeeded here or there to some unquantifiable degree. (And that goal is still shared by the large group of Americans formerly known as Mormons.) One verse from the Sermon on the Mount that one practically never hears these days is "Be ye therefore perfect, even as your father which is in heaven is perfect" (Mt. 5.49). Apart from the President, most of us are leery of "perfection"; but not the Puritans, and for all the mixed results of their efforts, they deserve a certain basic respect. Hall concludes by stressing "the vitality of Puritan-style politics and social ethics at a moment in our national history when democracy is failing and a social ethics of 'community' is being jeopardized." To which one is tempted to utter, if not a full-throated, a least a quietly sympathetic *touché*!

David Nirenberg. Anti-Judaism: The Western Tradition. Norton, 2013. 610pp. $35

The history of anti-Semitism (i.e., Jew-hatred) has been more or less written, from the semi-legendary Second Book of Maccabees to the meticulous scholarship of writers like Leon Poliakov, Raul Hilberg or Saul Friedlaender. But any reader of its dismal, horrific pages will have wondered: how did this poisonous plant manage to grow in so many places--England after 1290, 14th century France, post-1492 Spain, Reformation Germany, and so on--where there were so few actual Jews? (Even in the Third Reich, Jews made up <0.75% of the population.)

Clearly, we are dealing here with something much more complex and elusive, if not perverse, than ordinary ethnic hostility. Why, for example, was the damning label "Jewish" pinned on Castilian Christian poets (1391–1430) by one another, on Catholics by Lutherans, by Protestant regicides on King Charles I, on Kant by Hegel, and on American capitalism by sociologist Werner Sombart (d. 1941)? What's going on?

The answer, according to David Nirenberg, a professor of Medieval History and Social Thought at the University of Chicago, is the pestilential spread of what he calls "anti-Judaism." Though its effects could be seen in 1st and 2nd century Alexandria, whose Greek citizens and Roman legions savaged and finally eliminated most of the Jewish "foreigners," it most crucial roots lie in early Christianity. For Paul and all the evangelists (in varying degrees), the Jewish majority that rejected Jesus represented stubbornness, (deliberate) blindness, bad faith, hypocrisy, fixation of the Law (as opposed to freedom), on the letter (as opposed to the "spirit"), on justice (as opposed to mercy), on materialism (as opposed to Christian otherworldliness), on wealth (as opposed to Christian renunciation), and so forth.

The anti-Judaism of the New Testament is acknowledge by all serious students of the Bible. But, of course, that didn't end when Judaism and its "daughter" religion went their separate ways after 70 CE. Christians made supersessionism an essential feature of their faith, and so it would remain for Justin Martyr, Eusebius, Ambrose, Jerome, and the bloodthirsty John Chrysostom, all the way to Thomas Aquinas, canonized rabble-rouser like Vincent Ferrer and popes like Pius IX. Amid all this unfettered bigotry, St. Augustine's position looks almost benign. Yes, God had condemned the Jews to be outcasts, but "to the end of ... time the continued preservation of the Jews will be a proof to believing Christians of the subjection merited by those who ... put the Lord to death." So Jews shouldn't be killed, but left to serve as living reminders of their own dreadful mistake. If only that demeaning view had become the norm!

In any case, anti-Judaism expanded far beyond the Church. When the Enlightenment began replacing religious paradigms with secular ones, unbelievers (Hobbes, Spinoza,

D'Holbach, Voltaire, et al.) and their heirs (Kant, Schopenhauer, Fichte, Marx) borrowed it for their own purposes and, as Christians had before them, used it to attack their (mostly gentile) enemies. If in the process, they also vilified living Jews (and they did), that was a minot downside to the advantage of employing such a time-honored, effective, and widely accepted calumny. The Protocols of the Elders of Zion and the Nuremberg Race Laws were waiting in the wings.

Nirenberg, however, doesn't argue for any simplistic causality, linking, say, Luther's "On the Jews and Their Lies" to the gates of Auschwitz. This is history of ideas; and, given the overdetermined nature of human behavior, Nirenberg would never claim the thoughts and writings, however twisted, mean, and careless, of however many intellectuals, shaped the course of events all by themselves. But the extraordinary persistence and virulence of anti-Judaism (once can find it in 19th century New England and contemporary Japan) is, to say the least, deeply unsettling.

Nirenberg's coverage of this tale of near-insanity is vast and comprehensive. He discusses Egyptian violence against Jews in the 5th century BCE (Egyptians on the island of Elephantine were angry at the feast of Passover, claiming it celebrated their destruction. He explains how Muhammad and early Islamic tradition drew upon anti-Judaism ("O you who believe! If you obey a party of the People of the Book, they will make you disbelievers after your belief" Q 3:100) both to define and exalt Islam and combat its enemies, Jewish and otherwise. He offers brilliant interpretation of that subtle anti-Judaic masterpiece, The Merchant of Venice ("the Christian triumph over Judaism consists in knowing not how to keep the oath and its symbolic forms but when, in the interests of love, to let them go"). He examines texts both familiar (Marx's "Bruno Bauer: The Jewish Question") and obscure (a virulent sermon by one Father Antoine-Pascal-Hyacinthe Sermet to a gathering near Toulouse in 1790). He is at home in the original languages (Hebrew, Greek, Latin, Arabic, German, etc.) of all the material he cites; and his own style is clear and lively, vigorous and measured.

One issue Nirenberg barely touches on is the possible link between the Hebrew Bible and anti-Judaism. The prophets (and that would include Moses and Joshua) are forever fulminating about the sins of Israel, especially idolatry, and threatening bitter retribution. (One study reported that 75% of all prophetic oracles were negative. Christians certainly made hay with such unsparing attacks, the notion of the "remnant," etc. So did the Jews unwittingly hand the world a deadly weapon it could wield against them.? It's worth noting that, unlike Christianity, Judaism lost patience with the whole institution of prophecy, whence the famous blast in Zechariah 13: 2-3: "I will remove from the land the prophets and the unclean spirit. And if any one again appears as a prophet, his father and mother who bore him will say to him, 'You shall not live, for you speak lies in the name of the LORD'; and his father and mother who bore him shall pierce him through when he prophesies."

Prophets were almost by definition adversaries of their people and all too prone to poetic exaggeration. The Tanakh is surely the most self-critical Scripture anywhere.

—Peter Heinegg

BOOK REVIEW

RELIGION AS WE KNOW IT: AN ORIGIN STORY

Religion As We Know It: An Origin Story.
By Jack Miles. W.W. Norton,
New York, NY 2020. xI + 152 pp.
$14.95 (paperback)

If anyone can define religion, surely distinguished Biblicist (pardon the outdated, but sensible term) Jack Miles can —along with his many readers, especially the smaller heroic corps who have trekked through sizable stretches of his gigantic 4,448-page *Norton Anthology of World Religions* (2014). But wait, the *Norton* covers only Hinduism, Buddhism, Daoism, Judaism, Christianity, and Islam, inevitably consigning thousands of lesser known "faiths," alive or extinct, to oblivion. And Miles, who cites some twenty-three different scholarly notions of religion, instantly makes clear that religion can't be univocally defined because it's not one distinct thing, as we see in the endless permutations of folk practices, languages, cultural traditions and histories that it has fused with.

Many religions don't even have a word for "religion" or their own variety of it (as the British baptized the Hindus with the umbrella-concept Hinduism). Plenty of religions have no personal God (Buddhism); and practically all religions evolve and change in major directions (e.g., the late, tiny traces of belief in the afterlife found in the Hebrew Bible, not to mention today's liberal Christian views of homosexuality). Too bad we can't just stick with the handy old triad of creed, code, and cult, as found, for instance, in the classic work Miles never mentions, Huston Smith's *The World's Religions* (originally *The Religions of Man*, 1958). Smith's first title, by the way, exposes a problem that the *Norton*, with its stunning array of theologies, cosmologies, and philosophies surveyed and explicated, hardly has the time to address: the overwhelming predominance of males as founders and licensed promulgators of religion. Nowadays Religious Studies may be, or may soon become, a majority-female discipline, like Comparative Literature; and that development has already revolutionized the field. But for the most part the men got there first— with more than a few deleterious results.

Miles's book is simply an expanded and more personal version of the "Concluding Unscholarly Postscript" (alluding to Kierkegaard, of course) that he ended the *Norton Anthology* with. His point there was that Christian Europe invented comparative religion, and thus provided the conceptual framework we westerners use to describe and discuss religions of any sort. The early Christian Fathers did something exceptional: they separated the three hitherto inextricable elements of religion, ethnicity, and culture: They took Yahweh, the Jewish Lord of history, radically refashioned his interaction with his people and the world, drastically transformed the Torah, and abandoned key notions like a sacred language, homeland, and specific Holy City—even while clinging to essential Jewish religious ideas, "including monotheism, revelation, covenant, scripture, sin, repentance forgiveness, salvation, prophecy, messianism, and apocalypticism." One is tempted to irreverently call this the boldest hijacking in religious history (akin, in a minor way, to what Virgil did to Homer). In any case, with the coming of the Renaissance and Enlightenment, Christian academics started to apply the tools of secular analysis to biblical texts and doctrines, drawing upon burgeoning advances in the *Wissenschaft* of ancient languages, history, archeology, etc.; and so religion became the "subject" we are likely to think of today, repeatedly coming to conclusions that alter or flatly contradict familiar ways of thinking about the Abrahamic religions. All the unspeakably vivid literal images and teachings of Scripture have been demythologized, but not necessarily disenchanted, into "religion as we know it." Sentimental regrets and Fundamentalist hankerings aside, there's no way back.

All this is interesting and convincing; but the best part of Miles's presentation is the account of his own brand of belief. He was a Jesuit seminarian for a decade (1960-1970), and is now an Episcopalian (and choir member). He's long since left the Thirty-Nine Articles behind (and had the audacity to compose a lengthy biography of God); so whence does he approach institutional Christianity now (and with such enthusiasm)? Perhaps surprisingly, he cites Robert N. Bellah's *Religion in Human Evolution* (2011) for a crucial, often neglected source of religion: the instinct of *PLAY*.

That would explain a lot of things: the use of marvelous, but not literally credible, fictions, the intrinsic and often jovial communality of religious services, the artificial (supernatural) worlds conceived by play (creed), the frequency of precisely determined rules of the game (code), the curious, elaborate ways of performing ceremonies and "fooling around" (cult, a feature it shares with sports). And one could readily attach to religious play the related realms of Song and Dance. Is God's existence itself a sublime form of play that worshipers admire and participate in?

Miles extends such reflections (without necessarily naming or following upon them) by borrowing from Kwame Anthony Appiah's *As If: Idealization and Ideals* (2017), which in turn takes its inspiration from German philosopher Hans Vaihinger (1852-1933)'s *The Philosophy of "As If."* "It must be remembered," Vaihinger wrote, "that the object of the world of ideas as a whole is not the portrayal of reality—this would be an utterly impossible task—but rather to provide an *instrument for finding our way about more easily in the world.*" In this pious version of pragmatism, the 'useful untruths" of religion serve as indispensable guides to life, which is too unimaginably vast to be comprehended by and constrained in one flawlessly accurate "big picture." A familiar example of such an untruth would be the Virgin birth or Thomas Jefferson's idealistic phantasm that "all men are created equal, ... endowed by their Creator with certain unalienable rights": a patently false (by empirical standards) statement that nonetheless could be, and sometimes has been, a key to opening treasure houses of both charity and social opportunity. For a non-religious contemporary instance of this, Miles cites Michael Bloomberg's donation of $1.8 billion to Johns Hopkins, thereby assuring free tuition to all present and future students. As for his own stance, he summarizes it with a brief piece by Japanese poet Saigyō Hōshi (1118-1190) "On Visiting the Grand Shrine at Ise":

> Gods here?
> Who can know?
> Not I.
> Yet I sigh
> and tears flow
> tears on tears.

(N.B. Ignatius Loyola, Miles's former spiritual master, was a devoutly prodigious weeper and used to spend hours lying on the roof of the Gesù, the Jesuit headquarters in Rome, staring up at the starry night sky, dissolved in ecstatic tears—the polar opposite of Pascal's *libertin*, who was famously terrified by the eternal silence of infinite space.)

Of course, the "as if" theory of religious runs into a grand, not to say enormous, body of difficulties, starting with the mortalist's objection that both humans and their splendid religious cultures are doomed to disappear, as in Bertrand Russell's eloquent essay, "A Free Man's Worship," which demands acceptance of the fact that ultimately "the whole temple of man's achievement must inevitably be buried beneath the debris of a universe in ruins." That dire vision can no more be definitively proved or disproved than the blissful conclusion to the scenario of Sacred History; but anyone siding with Russell might be tempted to write off Miles as a tender-minded William Jamesian fideist. If so, he remains a fabulously well-informed, open-minded, and multi-faceted one. Friedrich Nietzsche, a fierce critic of Christianity (but certainly not of Greek paganism and various other religious *Weltanschauungen*) would insist that there is no pure Platonic essence of "religion," only religions as we know them, i.e., as interpreted by people with prefabricated schemata, e.g., members of the American Academy of Religion. But there's no necessary harm in that. And if such interpreters can also, like Miles, earnestly and joyfully play the game of faith, so much the better.

—Peter Heinegg

BOOK REVIEW

AN EMOTIONAL HISTORY OF DOUBT

An Emotional History of Doubt. By Alec Ryrie. Belknap Press of Harvard University Press, Cambridge, MA 2019. 262 pp. $27.95.

The standard genesis of modern western atheism, recently highlighted by the emergence of the likes of (who else?) Richard Dawkins, Christopher Hitchens, Daniel Dennett, and Sam Harris, et al., sees it as the product, first of the Renaissance and its celebration of pre-Christian antiquity, most notably the influence of the work of Epicurus and Lucretius. More to the point, historians generally stress the rise of science and the Enlightenment as a whole, with the usual suspects such as Spinoza, Voltaire, Diderot, Hume, and the Utilitarians, culminating inevitably in Nietzsche. But Ryrie, Professor of the History of Science at Durham University (and a self-confessed "believer with a soft spot for atheism), tries a different approach. He takes as his epigraph Julian Barnes's remark in *The Sense of an Ending* (2011), "Most of us, I suspect... make an instinctive decision, then build up an infrastructure of reason to justify it. And call the result common sense." In other words, the progression to both belief and unbelief is not a rational venture, an orderly kind of religious—or anti-religious—sorites, but an instinctual, emotional development, for which we later build one of Barnes's sincere, but after the fact rational explanations.

More specifically, Ryrie traces the rise of atheism in northern Europe to the Reformers' attack on Catholic orthodoxy and practice. Nowhere was fusillade of criticism and creative innovation more intense (and, at times, more bizarre) than in England; so Ryrie concentrates on English theologians and churchmen in the late sixteenth century and the turbulent period of 1640 to 1660 (with its sometimes antic cast of Levelers, Ranters, Quakers, Fifth Monarchists, Muggletonians, etc.). And could this have been a major line of thought leading to the death of God?

Contrary to the contemptuous, mocking stance and tone of today's atheists, he looks for the roots of atheism not in cold-eyed militant secularism or aggressive rationalism, but in "two interwoven emotional stories, of *anger* and *anxiety*." His case, more sketched out than minutely developed a mere 200 pages here seems to make *prima facie* case that the proverbial oceans of ink spilled in recent centuries by writers vehemently trying but failing to settle once and for all the question of God's existence show us that this is not primarily an intellectual enterprise? Tastes are deeply felt sensations; and the old saw still holds, *De gustibus non est disputandum*. And the New Atheists haven't even managed to impress many academic philosophers, who hold their popularizing brethren in mild, or not so mild, disdain.

Perhaps they just don't want their atheism *that shaggy*.

The Protestant Reformation unleashed a tsunami of anger, in language often both furious and foul, against the corrupt beliefs and practices of Rome—and before too long those of competing denominations as well. From there it was a logical leap to attack the very Deity presiding over the whole scheme, though writers couldn't say that out loud for many year.

Anxiety, says Ryrie, originally derived from "the unsettling, reluctant inability to keep a firm grip" on doctrines consciously believed to be true. Descartes (unmentioned by Ryrie) used his methodical doubt like a sort of well-trained retriever, who could track down and capture difficult issues, without ever getting violent about it. (There was no way his supposedly unsparing methodical doubt was going to destroy the Holy of Holies.) But the hounds of later religious philosophers were a fiercer breed of hunter.

What Christian writers in the Renaissance meant by "atheism" was not so much unbelief, but acting immorally, as if there was no God (and no afterlife to fear for one's transgressions). John Bunyan's Atheist sadly recounts how he searched for the supernatural world, and having to his great sadness not found it, he set off to find however much previously avoided sin he could commit. Ryrie's topic, then, is not about embracing or rejecting a doctrinal belief, but observing religious practices, adhering to "specifically religious ethics," and participating in an "avowedly religious community." People who tried to do these things, but didn't or couldn't, were de facto unbelievers

For Ryrie, atheism in the Middle Ages was something like shameless open immorality, call it a contemptuous form of mortalism (blasphemy, hatred of the clergy, dismissal of miracles, etc. "Unbelief," wrote Sir Thomas Browne (1605-1682) "was the general scandal of my profession." But evidence for this is scarce. Browne himself had his own idiosyncratic Baroque version of faith (and no scruples about burning witches at the stake). But elsewhere seeds of trouble were growing. Machiavelli's *Discourses on Livy* (1517) praised religion in the ancient Roman mode as a vital institution for preserving a civilized state. On the contrary, in *The Prince (1516)*—but not published till 1532, five years after his death–religion is treated as s sociopolitical tool: an essential element in running the state, not the guide to meaning of life. Unlike Roman paganism, Christianity weakened the state. Machiavelli wanted Christianity replaced by "something more muscular and (to be plain) more manly." Nietzsche, who admired the greater "masculinity" of Islam would have agreed. Of course, technically speaking, this amounts to atheism. But ironically in the "social, political, and emotional history of unbelief" intellectual denial of God was peripheral rather than central because most modern forms of atheism place even more stress on the core Christian virtue of mercy, even if they don't use the word.

Machiavelli made a major contribution to modern atheism by his concentration on Lucretius' doctrine of chance and the denial of the immortality of the soul. In a piquant contrast Erasmus held that Christians were the ultimate Epicureans because they thought the goal of human life was happiness; and true (eternal) happiness can be found only in virtue, making them consistent eudaemonists.

On the other hand, if Christianity was all about ethics (as opposed to, say, sacramental experience), hadn't many pre-Christian pagans been highly virtuous and religious? (Erasmus liked to say, *Saint Socrates pray for us*?) And in that case, however exalted an example Jesus was, could he be strictly speaking "necessary"? (Or, impious as it sounds, were the Prophets any more than eloquent, imaginative expositors of the Law?) For that matter, wasn't a good life perfectly possible without God?

Erasmus loyally stayed in the Church while mocking its superstitious and idolatrous practices. Bu the radical innovations of at least some Reformers would go much farther; and that left large and perilous room for uncertainty. How could believers be sure they were being true to the Gospel, were living, as the Catholics put it, in the "state of grace," and on the path to salvation? Rational criticism of "heathenish" practices and beliefs (infant baptism, the cult of the saints, pilgrimages, ancient myths and legends) could and eventually did descend into iconoclastic frenzy and rejection of all, or almost all, traditional ceremonies, formulas, and sacramentals—symbolized perhaps by huge piles of smashed stained glass?

And lastly mightn't all this lead to naked unbelief? (For many it obviously did.) As Montaigne (d. 1592) wrote,

Once you have put into their hands (the common people) the foolhardiness of despising and criticizing opinions ... and once you have thrown into the balance of doubt and uncertainly any articles of their religion, they soon cast all the rest of their beliefs into similar uncertainty. (tr. M.A. Screech)

Montaigne lived during (and almost lost his life in) the religious wars between Catholics and the Huguenots in late Sixteenth-century France; and so one can appreciate why this supreme skeptic (his famous motto being "Que sais-je?") would dislike religious unrest. But Ryrie goes too far in labeling Montaigne a believer. He was an Epicurean, a Pyrrhonist, a dedicated classicist-humanist, with no faith whatsoever in the afterlife. He did die while attending mass in his sick bed at the moment of the elevation; but he behaved in these matters as Horace or any of his Roman worldling friends would attend the official religious festivals of the state: as a civic duty, not an expression of "devotion."

Protestants had a field day attacking the more arcane features of Catholic theology, such as transubstantiation, Mariolatry, clerical and papal supremacy, mandatory celibacy, Purgatory and limbo (unmentioned in the New Testament), etc. But where was this critical earthquake to stop? It was no accident that the most learned and thorough German thinkers of the Reformation laid the groundwork for "Higher Criticism" and the faithless discipline of biblical studies.

Ryrie sees Montaigne as the father of fideism (later "weaponized" against Protestantism by Montaigne's successors). But while his position can be written off as an irenic live-and-let-live compromise, it can also be seen as a profoundly irrational leap in the dark. It's curious that Kyrie never mentions Montaigne's longest and most spirited theological work, "The Apology for Raymond Sebond." (II, 12) which is often celebrated as the nec plus ultra of "Christian skepticism." (In some graphic sections of the essay Montaigne describes various forms animal intelligence as superior to the human, suggesting that that, *pace* the Scholastics, theology is at bottom no "science" at all. Imagine tying to explain "Christian skepticism" to St. Paul or Augustine.

These are tricky territories to survey. Isn't there a destructive fury in Calvin's assault on Catholicism that could be seen as spilling over onto any kind of orthodox Christian theology? And what to make of Browne's simultaneous flirtation with both belief and unbelief in *Religio Medici*? Is Marlowe's Doctor Faustus a tragic hero or a supreme fool for playing a reversed type of Pascal's bet, and thereby suffering damnation? Or do Faustus' slash-and-burn putdowns of orthodoxy not strongly suggest that the whole mythic fantasy of selling one's soul for pleasure (Faustus mostly engages in silly misbehavior) is a joke—once again we hear echoes of Lucretius' brisk dismissal of post-mortem existence?

So, in a certain basic sense the roots of modern atheism lay in .... Protestantism. "Protestantism's entire doctrine of authority was compressed between the Bible's cover, and that was a difficult job of containment at the best of times ... If you could not uncomplicatedly trust that the Bible was God's Word [and how exactly did you define *that*?], the reading it was utterly changed. Thoughts and doubts about the text's meaning was a "woodworm quietly eating away the crossbeams of your faith." Hence the quintessential doubt and anxiety bedeviling modern faith.

Ryrie points to Hobbes and Spinoza as the archetypal founders of modern atheism, even though neither strictly qualified as such and (naturally) never embraced the term. The final section of *Leviathan* (1561) savagely strafed the Catholic Church and exploded biblical authority. But since secular governments enjoyed absolute authority, and absolute religious truth is unknowable, that same secular government could rightly have the final say on all matters of religion. Spinoza too demolished the supreme authority of Scripture and completely denied the possibility of miracles, thus leaving the world as remote from any kind of divine intervention on humans' behalf as Epicurus and Lucretius did.

The history of religious conflicts, of faith and doubt, of theism and atheism and all related subjects—which in one way or another constituted the theme of most of the books and pamphlets published in the western world till at least the mid-18th century—thus turns out, as Ryrie sees it, into a cosmic emotional psychomachia. And how not? Faith-based certainty might be compared to the gleaming surface of a frozen lake. One skates in speedy delight across the silvery surface—until one hears an ominous crack and one's foot gets either lightly snagged or deeply stuck in the ice. (Call it the uh-oh. as opposed to the aha, experience: one existentially realizes the depth and danger of the enormous liquid mass beneath one. The brilliance of Ryrie's book is the vast company of writers, from the famous and familiar (John Bunyan, Robert Burton, Christopher Marlow, Richard Hooker, Walter Raleigh, etc.) to the more or less obscure figures (to non-specialized readers anyhow) like Mary Springett, Caspar Schwenckfeld, Dirck Volkesetz Coornhert, William Waldwyn, Eleazar Duncan, and so on) that he assembles and conducts in a sort of rich but jagged harmony.

However elegantly told, the moral of the story is simplicity itself: leaving a safe, steady, religious position for what looks like an exciting and a dramatic one resembles St. Peter's fabled attempted to follow Jesus' bidding and walk on the Sea of Galilee is bound to be a highly "emotional" experience. i.e., more fearful than ecstatic, at least at first. And the possibility always remains, in one way or another, of going under, or, to change the metaphor, having to climb the fearsome mountains described by Gerard Manly Hopkins ("Frightful, sheer, no-man-fathomed. Hold them, cheap/ May who ne'er hung there," No worst, there is none.) Ryrie's characterization of unbelief is a provocative and convincing one that readers situated at any point of the spectrum of faith or doubt or both will have something to learn from.

—Peter Heinegg

CROSSCURRENTS AT 48

Charles Henderson

On the occasion of our 70th anniversary, I present these words from our founding editor, Joseph Cunneen, originally presented at our 48th anniversary celebration, as he was retiring. It gives a vivid sense of the excitement surrounding the launch of this journal as well as highlights of the publication during his nearly 50 years as editor. It also traces, in brief, the history of the journal through its merger with the Association for Religion and Intellectual Life and its journal: Religion and Intellectual Life.

Looking back at *Cross Currents* after forty-eight years as editor and co-editor requires an effort to disentangle the personal story of a small group of friends from developments in both the church and the world since World War II. The record of what we published gives me considerable satisfaction but a moment's reflection makes it clear that we were not makers of history but excited and surprised participants in a process of rapidly accelerating change.

Seed for the earliest idea of the magazine was first sown by John Julian Ryan, while teaching an advanced writing course I took at Holy Cross College in 1942. He complained that there was really no first-class Catholic intellectual journal. One could be created, he maintained, by bringing together the best from existing reviews—and he offered as examples *Oratres Fratres* (publishing today as *Worship*) and *Theological Studies* in the United States, and *Dublin Review* and *Blackfriars* in England. The seed fell on poorly prepared ground. Ryan had captured my attention by reading us an essay by a German refugee priest-liturgist, H. A. Reinhold, "Inroads of the Bourgeois Spirit," from *Commonweal,* which I had at least heard of, but the other journals were new to me.

More than three years later, the surrender of the Germans in 1945 occasioned a special opportunity for me to learn something of European intellectual Catholicism. I had served in a combat engineer battalion with Patton's 3rd Army in the advance from Normandy to Czechoslovakia; on the assumption that many of us would still be needed in the war against Japan, all kinds of programs were started to keep troops usefully occupied. I was sent to Paris for seven weeks for a course in French Language and Civilization, an idyllic period in which, after morning classes, I was free to walk all over the city. There, too, I had a reunion with a close high school friend who had gotten a weekend pass from an air base in northern France and gave me a copy of *Esprit,* a French monthly I had never seen before. He told me that its editor, Emmanuel Mounier, was a committed Catholic, which surprised me, since the cover of the journal announced, "Marxism est un humanisme."

I was nevertheless intrigued with its contents, and, at age 22 still naive enough to walk over to rue Jacob the following Monday and ask to see the editor. The receptionist was a bit startled, but ushered me into Mounier's office while he was eating a spartan lunch at his desk. When he quickly insisted that *Esprit* was not a Catholic journal, I was taken aback. I wasn't yet prepared to understand how Mounier's personalism had led him to create a journal in which agnostics and people of different faith traditions raised fundamental political and religious questions in an atmosphere of mutual respect.

The background of *CrossCurrents* cannot be explained without a realization that the GI bill made graduate school a real possibility for a whole generation, including thousands of Catholics who previously could not have considered it. Discharged from the army in 1946, I attended Catholic University's flourishing School of Drama, and was sufficiently aware of my ignorance to try to take additional courses in theology. I earned my Master's degree with a thesis on the plays of Paul Claudel, but learned no theology because of graduate school policy at that time: no laity were admitted to theology courses, even as auditors.

The taste for Paris, as well as continuing curiosity about theology, next led me- after a brief experience on the stage as a member of Actor's

Equity- to use the GI Bill to take courses at the Institut Catholique in January 1948. There I was allowed to sit in on large lecture classes for which I was unprepared but could benefit, due to the practice of teachers distributing copious mimeographed notes. A relative pioneer as an ex-GI in the Institut's theology program, I was befriended by Fr. Louis Bouyer, who gave me an excellent introductory reading list, beginning with DeLubac's *Catholicisme*. I took endless notes on the books he recommended, and began to see important links between *Esprit,* Danielou's interreligious journal, *Dieu Vivant,* and the Dominican monthly, *La Vie Intellectuelle.* Even though I had no intention of working for a doctorate in theology, it was an educationally fruitful time; in addition to keeping up with contemporary French drama, I visited the offices of the JEC (Young Christian Students), where I was given treasured mimeographed pages by Teilhard de Chardin, and walked to Chartres with hundreds of other students on Pentecost weekend.

When I returned to New York to begin teaching in Fordham's theater department in September 1948, the idea that was to become *CrossCurrents* was given further stimulus by contacts with an impressive team of Catholic graduate students at the University of Chicago. The group, which included specialists in philosophy, physics, economics, sociology, political science, and literature, had been responsible for *Concord,* a lively YCS magazine aimed principally at undergraduates, and were laying plans for a more ambitious and sophisticated journal. Because of considerable experience with the National Student Association, and international contacts through participation in the first post-war convention of the YCS, they were so aware of why academe often found campus Christian groups arrogant and irrelevant that they questioned the wisdom of giving the proposed new quarterly any religious identification.

Several of the Chicago team came to New York early in 1949 for a weekend of discussion with New York friends who were interested, and in August I went out to Chicago to see if the vague idea was ready to take shape. I was hoping that the *Concord* veterans would use their experience and their mailing lists to produce a translation of important articles from European sources.

Although only a minority of the Chicagoans were familiar with the French journals that had excited me, discussion was never acrimonious. The problem, endemic to young groups, was how to keep them together;

would there be enough people who would commit the time and energy needed to make the new journal possible?

It soon became apparent that the majority had other responsibilities: two were getting married and moving to California, another was writing his dissertation and would be unavailable for at least a year, another was accepting a teaching position in another part of the country, etc. By the time I took the bus back to New York, I believed the journal was stillborn, even though I had asked Sally—who was travelling in France and England and whom I was to marry in November- to call on several European editors to facilitate permission to translate articles. Joe Caulfield, however, who was teaching humanities courses at Manhattan College, encouraged me to believe that with help from local friends who had shown interest, the magazine could be edited from New York. My mother-in-law even proposed its aptly open-ended name, and by the end of the year Sally probably believed that Cross Currents was part of the wedding contract. My New York associates, despite their many gifts, had no ideological agen da; unlike their French equivalents, they could not have fired off a manifesto before lunch. Nevertheless, they held some common attitudes and stressed some common issues, however broadly they might be conceived. These included a desire to move out of the largely self-imposed intellectual ghetto of an ear lier immigrant Catholic generation, with the intention of drawing on Christian resources to engage the wider culture. They had learned to be suspicious of clericalism, resisted the defensive, censor-prone mentality still dominant in the Catholic colleges of the time, and believed that if the call for lay participation in the church was to be genuine, there must be far better communication, a genuine sharing of responsibility, and a less top-down style of operation. They thought it important to look on Marx, Darwin, and Freud, to choose three examples, less as enemies than as thinkers to learn from. It will be noted that no one in either the Chicago team or among my New York friends was a theologian, and none of us had the least intention of starting a theological journal. At the same time, perhaps more than today when there are far more Catholic PhD's, we assumed that aspiring intellectuals in any field should be theologically informed. The original editors had widely varying interests and strengths: Erwin Geissman, who was teaching Renaissance English literature in Fordham's graduate school, was struck by the importance of John

Courtney Murray's work on church-state relations; Caulfield was fascinated with the implications of the unpublished Teilhard material; Alfred DiLascia, who was teaching philosophy at Manhattan, had become a disciple of the exiled Dom Luigi Sturzo during the latter's years in New York; and my interest in the French Catholic literary revival was deepened by translating several plays of Gabriel Marcel. Marie-Christine Hellin was employed at the UN on issues of prison reform; Leon King was also involved at the UN, but more informally, working with francophone African delegates who were seeking national independence; Ernst Winter, who was teaching politics at Iona College, was looking for constructive ways of breaking out of the cold war impasse; and Sally was trying to juggle motherhood with literary-philosophical research on the conflict of freedom and love in personal behavior.

Many others deserve to be mentioned, doing everything from sharing ideas and translating articles to addressing envelopes. What was most striking, however, about our efforts to prepare the way for CrossCurrents was the response we received from a range of distinguished figures who might not have been expected to give much encouragement to unknown young teachers with an untried idea. Reinhold Niebuhr and his wife Ursula invited Sally and me to small gatherings at their apartment at Union Theological Seminary whenever some eminent foreign visitor was coming through New York; Hannah Arendt gave me leads to European Christian journals she considered indispensable; George Shuster, then the president of Hunter College, shared his knowledge of German Catholicism and lessons of his long journalistic career; and George Florovsky, at St. Vladimiur's Seminary, reminded me of the riches of the Russian Orthodox tradition. Perhaps most important in terms of both practical help and enduring friendship, my brightest Jewish student at Fordham, when I wondered where to find a printer, sent me to Alexander Donat, a noble Polish Jewish printer-publisher who, with his wife and son, had survived the horrors of concentration camps and launched the Waldon Press in Greenwich Village. Donat not only showed notable patience with unpaid bills and corrected our omission of umlauts from German words, but would also predict, while a new issue was in page proofs, which article would elicit the most interest. His most important contribution, however, came late at night when the presses were quiet, his staff had gone home, and we were both exhausted; he would then raise the haunting question: how, after the horrors of the Nazi era, is one to believe? In one way, the launching of CrossCurrents—its first issue appeared in December 1950—was a quixotic adventure, but we were as fortunate as we were naive. After we had ordered the printing of 50,000 brochures in June 1950, Pius XII issued Humani Generis, an encyclical which seemed a head-on condemnation of much that we had promised to print in early issues. Suspicion became attached to terms like existentialism, evolution, and "the new theology": Henri DeLubac received a warning; Jean Danielou showed extra caution as to which of his essays could be translated, Yves Congar's Vraimet fausse reforme dans l'eglise was withdrawn from circulation, and Frank Sheed, in a fraternal gesture, cautioned us not to publish Teilhard in the near future.

Nevertheless, the long insulation of Catholic thought by means of a coercive anti-modernism was no longer possible. Though there was a cloud over a good number of the writers we were to publish in the 50s, this also meant there was less competition for the right to reproduce their essays, and CrossCurrents soon became known as the place to look for an English-language reflection of the most advanced and interdisciplinary European Christian thought.

What we had stumbled into—to our credit, we were actively searching out such material to give a deeper grounding to our own faith—was the harvest of long pre pared projects like Edition du Cerf's Unum Sanctam series on the church, the Barthian challenge to an earlier Protestant liberalism, and the lessons drawn by survivor-participants of resistance to totalitarian Fascism and Communism. As can easily be appreciated, such resistance- in terms of both political activism and scholarly reflection on the scandal of "divided Christendom" (a phrase used as a title for one of Congar's Unam Sanctam studies)—prepared minds and hearts for an ecumenism that had not yet found public expression in the United States.

The first issue (Fall 50), which appeared in December 1950, contained a brief editorial which stated that "our primary function will be to reprint outstanding articles from foreign and out-of-the-way sources that indicate the relevance of religion to the intellectual life." After stating our hope of drawing on non-European sources, it called for an end to Western domination of Asia and Africa and offered a sober reminder to U.S. readers: "our best friends all over the world are watching our country critically .. America has not yet convinced them that she has a spiritual message with which to rally free men."

The conclusion was concise: "Because we are Catholics, we welcome contributions to the truth from any source; we must try to find out—Christians and non-Christian together—what it might mean to be a Christian today." The lead article was Mounier's "Christian Faith and Civilization"; it was followed by Emil Brunner's "The Christian Sense of Time," Nicolas Berdyaev's "Christianity and Anti-semitism," and Franz Schoeningh's "What is Christian Politics?," as well as Marcel's "Theism and Personal Relationships," and DeLubac's essay on Marxist and Christian man.

Not long after, I was asked to see the president of Fordham, and naively believed that I was to be commended for showing faculty initiative. Instead, I was asked what would be my response to a request that *CrossCurrents* submit to prior censorship. There had been no official complaint about the journal, the president told me, but the chancery office was apparently curious about the fact that its editor was teaching at the university. The president remained polite and made no demands; it was clear that he merely wanted to protect Fordham from embarrassment in case questions about orthodoxy were raised later. He had already secured an opinion from a canon lawyer, who soberly pointed out that there was not much work for a censor to do in this case: several of the articles we had included—including that by the Protestant theologian Emil Brunner—had first appeared in French Jesuit journals where material was already submitted to such oversight. The interview ended with neither defiance on my part nor insistence by the president; I could not help feeling, however, that there was something unhealthy in the fact that I was left with no record of the meeting to bring to my fellow-editors, and even without have a copy of the canon lawyer's report. The vague cloud dissolved: there were friendly Jesuits at Fordham who worked out some formula that promised to insulate the university against the charge of laxity. Indeed, in the context of the time, McCarthyism—and its attendant anti-Communist hysteria—was a more immediate threat. This may be why several eyebrows were raised when our second issue contained Karl Barth's "The Church between East and West," which refused to give an uncritical blessing to "our" side. Overall reaction was enthusiastic, however, because of articles by Romano Guardini on myth and revelation, Marcel More on Graham Greene's The Heart of the Matter, Martin Buber on "the education of character," Danielou's "dialogue with time," and two subtle French Jesuit essays—by Jean Rimaud and Louis Beirnaert, on psychiatry, morality, and holiness. There had been only 300 subscribers when the first issue was printed. By the end of the first year there were 1700. John Cogley wrote a complimentary column on the journal in *Commonweal* in 1951, and *Christian Century* gave a rave review to the 1954 bound volume, saying, "Every article, every review, is of interest to Christians." Readers were responsive to the range of topics and viewpoints, from a dense historical analysis of church and state by John Courtney Murray to Simone Weil's "Beyond Personalism," Friedrich Heer on the French priest-workers, Jean Lacroix on the meaning of contemporary atheism, Augustin Leonard's "The Christian and the non-Christian," Henri Dumery's "The Temptation to do good," Paul Ricoeur's "Morality without sin or sin without moralism?," Karl Rahner's "Church of Sinners," Paul Tillich's "Jewish influences on Protestant theology," Guardini on Dostoyevsky's Idiot, Congar's "True and False Reform," Buber's "Guilt and Guilt Feelings," Niebuhr on the cold war, and Cardinal Newman's "On Consulting the Faithful in Matters of Doctrine."

They also appreciated the fact that not all articles had explicit "religious" concerns but were chosen because they dealt seriously with topics on which the U.S. media of the day left us inadequately informed: the economics of third-world countries, the problem of nuclear weapons, the emergence of an independent Africa, the media revolution, ethics and population control. Philosophers were impressed by a pluralistic parade of essays by such leading figures as Jaspers, Husserl, Merleau-Ponty, Blondel, Pieper, and Maritain, and by the exhaustive annual surveys of Philosophy by James Collins. And at a time when psychoanalysis was frequently condemned by religious spokesmen there were enough articles on religion and psychiatry to fill a first-rate anthology.

The journal's greater self-confidence manifested itself in the inclusion of more articles by North American authors, including Bernard Lonergan, Rosemary Ruether, Krister Stendahl, John McDermott, Gregory Baum, Eugene Fontinell, Arnold Jacob Wolf, William Birmingham, and David O'Brien. By 1958 there was a new pope in Rome, John XXIII, but the editors did not immediately perceive the possibilities he opened up when he almost immediately called an ecumenical council. After a worldwide request went out for statements of Christian aspirations, however, interest soon quickened. As the opening of Vatican II approached, we translated a half-dozen articles from a special issue of *Esprit*, added a few U.S. contributors, and produced "Looking Toward the Council" (Spring 62), bringing together the concerns of Catholic, Protestant, and Eastern Orthodox Christians on several continents. The explosion of demands in the 60s inevitably found reflection in the review. In terms of church structures, Piet Fransen explained episcopal councils as a way to reduce excessive centralization in Catholic decision-making. On a more human level, the deep frustration of lay Catholics at Paul VI's decision to remove birth control from Vatican IPs agenda found a reflective outlet in 1964 with Louis Dupre's sober re-examination of underlying issues in that debate. A many-faceted look at the wider subject, "Sexuality and the modern world," was drawn from another special issue of *Esprit*; Francis Simon offered a bishop's open-ended discussion of "the new morality," and the narrower question of the acceptability of married priests was carefully addressed by R. J. Bunnik in a two-part historical-theological essay. Of much wider import, Rosemary Ruether's "The Becoming of Women in Church and Society" (1967) raised feminist issues to which society was beginning to listen and the Catholic hierarchy still preferred to ignore. In international terms, U.S. policy in Vietnam was exposed in a 1965 analysis of the "Viet Cong" and Francois Houtart examined the war in the light of "Populorum Progressio," Paul VI's encyclical on development. Tissa Balasuriya dramatized growing third-world impatience in "World Apartheid," and in 1968 James Lamb guest-edited "For White America," a special issue that challenged both colonialism and Western assumptions about human needs. But even in that terrible year of assassinations and disillusionment, CrossCurrents was able, with the assistance of yet another guest-editor, Walter Capps, to produce a symposium on the theology of hope.

Prompt translation by David Abalos of key documents from the 1968 Medellin conference of Latin American bishops gave readers a head start in understanding the turmoil in Latin America that grew increasingly dramatic in the next decade. Gary MacEoin guest-edited a special issue on liberation theology in 1971, introducing the work of Gustavo Gutierrez and providing a needed historical and political context.

Articles by liberationists like J-L Segundo, Jon Sobrino, and Leonardo Boff soon followed, as well as Archbishop Romero's declaration on the church, political organization, and violence, which we published just before he was murdered. The power of Christian "base communities" was illuminated by Frei Betto's declaration, "The church we want," and the Brazilian movement was carefully analyzed by L. Deelen. J-B. Metz's "Redemption and Emancipation" and Dorothee Solle's "Christianity and socialism" indicated parallel developments in European political theology.

American intellectual provincialism was further challenged by "The Good Red Road," an issue devoted to Native American literature and religion and edited by Mary Louise Birmingham, as well as other special issues on Sri Aurobindo, (edited by Robert McDermo Birmingham, as well as other special issues on Sri Aurobindo, (edited by Robert McDermott), Africa, and the cross-cultural and religious research of Raimon Panikkar. Parig Digan's lengthy analysis of his torical relations between "China and the churches" was equally mind-stretch ing. The Spring 1977 issue brought together articles by James Cone, Shawn Copeland, Joyce Erickson, and Beatrice Bruteau, revealing parallel concerns in black and feminist theology, while Beverly Harrison's "The New Consciousness of Women" and Elizabeth Schussler-Fiorenza's "Early Christianity in a Feminist Perspective" compelled recognition of feminist theological maturity. If the underlying ferment of the decade was best put in per spective by Michel DeCerteau's "Revolutions in the Believeable," the 1974 double issue on world spirituality, "Word out of Silence," edited by John-David Robinson, bringing together Chistians, Jews, Hindus, Buddhists, and Sufis, received the most enthusiastic response.

The 80's gave initial welcome to "The Personalism of John Paul II," by John Hellman, and saw special issues on the international peace movement, gender, Dorothy Day and the Catholic Worker, and Jacques Ellul. While conflict with Rome over liberation theology, and with Washington's repressive policies in Central America, were recurring topics—as seen in articles by Anselm Min and Jan Black, room was made for the introduc tion of previously unknown European writers ? Brigitta Trotzig, by Adma d'Heurle, and Jean Sulivan, by Padraig Gormally. Georges Khodr looked closely at scriptural ambiguities in "The Gospel and Violence," Rene Girard saw "The Gospel Passion as Victim's Story," and Raymond Brown tried to preserve the gains of Catholic biblical criticism from extremist interpreters. Vincent Harding called for a genuine inclusiveness in his "open letter on Habits of the Heart," and interreligious exchange was expanded by Aloysius Pieris' magiste rial essay on Christian-Buddhist dialogie, as well as by a group of 1985 articles by Leonard Swidler, Jacob Neusner, Anton Ugolnik, Notto Thelle, and Beatrice Bruteau. Probably the most significant development in the journal during the 80s was increased awareness of the religious dimension of the ecological movement, best expressed in the special section of the Summer-Fall issue devoted to the work of Thomas Berry, including three key essays? "Creative Energy," "The New Story" and "Dream of the Earth." Another special issue, "Revisioning Philosophy," asked Western philosophers to stretch their understanding to include Eastern thought. Raimon Panikkar raised a crucial further question: can Christians claim both chosenness and universality? As William Birmingham, co-editor since 1985, insisted, "To read his essay...as an exercise in negative criticism would be mistaken. Panikkar has written instead a prolegomenon to Christian self-understanding."

1990 meant a happy alliance with the Association for Religion and Intellectual Life (ARIL), which produced the practical benefits of a third co-editor, Nancy Malone, O.S.U. (who had previously edited the Association's quarterly, Religion and Intellectual Life), and an office at the College of New Rochelle (through the kindness of Sister Dorothy Ann Kelly, O.S.U., the college's dynamic president).

The fact that ARIL was a Christian-Jewish association made it easier to attract a new group of Jewish scholars to write for CrossCurrents, extending the dialogue fostered in previously published essays by Elie Wiesel, Emil Fackenheim, Emmanuel Levinas, Jacob Neusner, Arthur Cohen, and Eugene Borowitz, as well as Krister Stendahl's call for a new relationship between Judaism and Christianity. The inaugural joint issue, Spring 1990, concentrated on Jewish-Christian subjects, with contributions on Jewish-Christian marriage, an exchange on liberation theology, and Lawrence Hoffman's irenic discussion of the possibilities of common worship. The Summer issue included the major papers of ARIL's consultation on faith commitment and intellectual disciplines, including papers by Edith Wyschogrod, Robert Wuthnow, David O'Brien, Richard Niebuhr, and Denise Levertov, and Fall added a further interreligious perspective in Riffat Hassan's "What does it mean to be a Moslem today?"

The following years saw a wide variety of special issues—on the "Return to Scripture," "The Once and Future University," interdisciplinary perspectives on the self, ecotheology, esthetics and religion, "Spiritualities in a post-Einsteinian universe," science and religion, and new feminist theologies. Readers seemed to find that a new feature, interviews, with David Tracy, John Polkinghorne, Bishop Rowan Williams, and John Dominic Crossan, offered helpful introductions to major figures and complex questions. Since there was no way to avoid the subject of post-modernism, the journal presented diverse approaches: Peter Ochs' essay on Eugene Borowtiz and Jewish postmodernist philosophy, a theological analysis by Daniel J. Adams, a Protestant professor in Korea, and the e-mail exchange between Edith Wyschogrod and John D. Caputo.

At the merger of ARIL with CrossCurrents Nancy Malone expressed her vision of "creating for the first time in the United States an avowedly interfaith journal that will be a voice for our country's entire religiously and morally engaged intellectual community." The editors, she said, "are committed to breaking the silence about religion in the intellectual life of the United States, to show that religion is liberating, that it has a central place in discussion of hunger, of ecology, of every social issue. We hope, in particular, to inject religion into the overwhelmingly a-religious conversation of higher education."

Despite the outreach of ARIL's annual convocation, its month-long Colloquium for younger scholars, and scattered success with local discussion groups devoted to related ends, at retirement in 1997 she would probably have claimed only modest gains toward such goals. Not that she or her co-editors aren't proud of the publication record of those years: a hefty anthology could be made up of the best of the 1990s, perhaps opening with Eugene Pogany's powerful 1995 memoir of twin brothers—his Jewish father and priest-uncle, separated by faith after the Holocaust. Other essays I would nominate for such a volume include that of Mary Boys on whether the cross can be reclaimed as a Christian symbol, David Tracy on the hidden God, Brenda Meehan on wisdom/sophia, Russian identity, and feminism, Jacob Neusner's "There has never been a Jewish-Christian dialogue—but there could be one," Marie Sabin's analysis of the representation of women in Mark's Gospel, David Toolan's "Praying in a post-Einsteinian universe," Albert Raboteau's reflections on African American history, and Sandra Schneider's discussion of the possible transfiguration of religious life.

Lists make boring reading or I would be tempted to continue, exploiting the names of even better-known authors. More useful, however, would be to suggest gains and omissions. An opening to positive resources in Islam, as in Khalid Duran's Winter 1992-3 essay on an alternative to Islamism, represented a real advance in interreligious understanding, as did Pravajika Vrajaprana's discussion of "What do Hindus do?" and Leo Lefebure's probing of related concerns in the work of Masao Abe and Karl Rahner.

On the other hand, the emergence of the United States as the one unchallenged world power, coupled with the dehumanizing consequences of economic liberalism in the emerging world economy, did not find comparable indepth discussion. Everyday editorial frustration, however, as well as a slow loss in circulation, has probably been due more to the difficulty of an interreligious journal communicating a sense of clear identity. There is genteel approval of our good intentions, but also a widespread sense among Catholics, Protestants, and Jews alike that it is not "their" publication. The problem is intensified at present because intellectuals in all these groups are discouraged by internal losses and divisiveness. Since CrossCurrents began as an ecumenically-oriented initiative of Roman Catholics, it is appropriate to conclude with a brief comment on the situation in the church, presently dominated by the restorationist impulses of a papacy that speaks of human rights for everyone but Catholic intellectuals. The Curia may well feel they can do without theologians, but the church can hardly thrive when millions of its best-informed and committed women are deeply alienated. No attack on papal authority could have done as much damage to its prestige as John Paul II's insistence that the church is not free to consider the ordination of women.

Only a tiny percentage of women seek ordination for themselves, but all of us, men and women alike, are capable of getting the point of Joseph Blenkinsopp's 1995 essay, that what is "at stake in the non-ordination of Roman Catholic women" is power, not theology. The situation has extra pathos because John Paul II is brilliant, prayerful, and charismatic— as well as very ill. But this does not reduce the harm done by a disregard for tradition in the appointment of subservient bishops, or in contradicting lofty declarations of support for the poor by turning over dioceses to the Opus Dei. As for Cross Currents, it will inevitably change to reflect new developments, but such change will most likely be incremental. In any case, Rome's difficulty in surmounting the strictures of celibate clericalism should not distract Catholic intellectuals from continuing to read and write for CrossCurrents, while redoubling their efforts to interiorize their faith and to avoid reducing the Gospel to ideology.

    Joseph Cunneen
    Founding Editor

CROSSCURRENTS
A BRIEF HISTORY OF THE RESEARCH COLLOQUIUM

Charles Henderson

The month-long research colloquium has, in addition to the journal, been at the very center of the mission of ARIL. The following, short history highlights the origins of the colloquium in Boston and traces its evolution in the early years as it moved first to Yale University, then Columbia University, and most recently to Auburn Seminary in New York where it currently resides. Each year ARIL brings scholars from around the world to work on research projects of their own design around a common theme.

The idea of a colloquium, a month-long opportunity for scholars from varying back-grounds and disciplines to come together for research and writing in an atmosphere of critical thinking and supportive relationships, evolved from the Faculty Forum. The Faculty Forum was part of the work of the Episcopal Church Society for College Work and later the National Institute for Campus Ministry.

The Colloquium was funded by William Coolidge and began in 1984, the first summer following the organization that then called itself the Associates for Religion and Intellectual Life (ARIL). Among its early leaders were Myron Bloy, and Episcopal priest and executive director of ARIL, Nancy Malone, a Roman Catholic religious, and Johnny Crocker who was at the time chaplain at MIT. These folks worked hand in hand with Mary Sargent, Mr. Coolidge's personal secretary in shaping the program. Coolidge, an Episcopalian and sometime member of the Board of Trustees of the Episcopal Divinity School in Cambridge, Massachusetts, was eager to support the work of integrating religious conviction with academic and intellectual activity.

The first Colloquium was held June 11 to July 7, 1984, at the Episcopal Divinity School. The director was Tony Stoneburner, then Professor of English Literature at Dennison University, Granville, Ohio. Tony was ably assisted by Chaplain-Theologians from Jewish, Catholic, and Protestant traditions. In the first year, these consisted of Joseph Holland, Richard Levy, and Stanley Hauerwas.

Twenty four Fellows comprised the 1985 Coolidge Research Colloquium, held at Andover-Newton Theological School, June 9 to July 5. Tony Stoneburner continued as Director for this second year. His report illustrates both similarity to the first year and dramatic difference: "Last year there was only one Jewish Fellow, this year half-a-dozen; last year no Fellow from Eastern Orthodoxy, this year one; last year no blacks, this year two. Last year a third of the Fellows were campus ministers; this year over three-quarters were academics." (*Ibid.*, p. 57)

"There was a difference of emphasis between academics and campus ministers: the former re-grounded themselves within their own religious traditions; the latter re-grounded themselves in study, scholarship, research. All engaged in deep ecumenical dialogue (not lease during ecumenical midrash-study)." (*Ibid.*) Richard Levy returned as a Resource Person or Theologian-in-Residence. He was joined by Ian Barbour.

The 1986 Colloquium was again held at the Episcopal Divinity School. Elizabeth and Melvin Keiser, respectively, professors of English and Religious Studies at Guilford College, were the directors. EDS as a site was thought to be ideal because of its resources and the availability of both the EDS and the Harvard libraries.

The Keisers returned in 1987 to direct the Colloquium for another year. "Like last year's, [it] was an extraordinarily rich experience, interweaving the spiritual, intellectual, and personal, which can perhaps only be best described in theological language: it is a time of grace." (*Religion & Intellectual Life*, Fall 1987, Vol V, No. 1, p.137). Mary Luke Tobin was the Catholic Resource Theologian for a second year; Richard Levy, the Jewish Resource Theologian, returned for his fourth year. The journal report on this year includes comments from several of the Fellows. The directors concluded that the Colloquium "can make a significant contribution from its unique strength of the experience of genuine community among Jews and Christians." (*Ibid.*, p. 138).

The 1998 Colloquium saw an increased emphasis on Jewish-Christian dialogue over that of the previous year. This was due to the fact that

Fellows "came with this explicitly on their agenda." This year also saw the addition of three new resource leaders.

"What's valuable is that the essential focus here is academic and intellectual; that religious questions and perspectives are admissible and intrinsic; that all this takes place in an interfaith, pluralistic context. The thing just works - it's a fantastic, unique concept in all ways - spiritually, intellectually, socially." (*Religion & Intellectual Life*, Fall 1988, Vol. VI, No. 1, p. 125). It is noteworthy that this issue of the Journal includes a tribute to William A. Coolidge, the benefactor of the Colloquium that bears his name. When Mr. Coolidge died in the mid-nineties, he left an endowment gift to assure the future of the Colloquium.

June 4 - 30, 1989 were the days of this year's Coolidge Research Colloquium. The Journal lists only the names of the Fellows and their projects. The directors were again the Keisers with resource leaders that included Jonathan Omer-Man, from the Los Angeles Hillel Council; Nancy Malone, O.S.U., from ARIL; and Jack Boozer, Professor of Religion, Emeritus, Emory University. Jack Boozer died in Amsterdam on July 19, 1989. My recollection is that the ARIL Newsletter was published this year and the Directors' Report was included in that publication.

The seventh annual Coolidge Research Colloquium was again held at EDS from June 10-July 9, 1990. It was a year of change both for the Colloquium and for the ARIL Journal. Our Journal merged with *Cross Currents*. It was a year of leveraged buy-outs, and we were not to be left out. Although the Colloquium was still held on the EDS campus, the directors changed: Elizabeth Kirk, Professor of English, Brown University, and Joan Lescinski, C.S.J., College of St. Rose, Albany, NY, served as co-directors. Jonathan Omer-Man and Nancy Malone returned as resource leaders. Also new this year was Henry F. Knight, Jr., Chaplain, Baldwin-Wallace College, Berea, OH, as Protestant Resource Leader.

In the years that follow reports of the Colloquium are found in the minutes of the Board of Directors and/or in the ARIL Newsletter. The Cross*Currents* Journal no longer carried reports, although essays and articles by several Fellows have been published over the years. In 1995, the locus of the Colloquium moved to Yale University, and a year later to Columbia University and Auburn Seminary where it currently resides.

CROSSCURRENTS
CONTRIBUTORS

Thomas J. Millay is a Senior Research Fellow at the Hong Kierkegaard Library, St. Olaf College, a Contributing Editor at the *Los Angeles Review of Books*, and the Pastor of First Christian Church, Goldsboro, NC. He is the author of *You Must Change Your Life: Søren Kierkegaard's Philosophy of Reading* (Cascade Press, 2020) and two books forthcoming in 2021, *Christian Asceticism: A Cascade Companion* (Cascade Press) and *Kierkegaard and the New Nationalism: A Reinterpretation of the Attack upon Christendom* (Lexington Press). He is currently researching how traditional practices of asceticism such as fasting, almsgiving, and vigils can be a resource for resistance to contemporary Christian nationalism.

tom.millay54@gmail.com

Eugene Trager is a Clinical Associate Professor of Psychiatry at the University of Illinois College of Medicine. He is a Diplomate of the American Board of Psychiatry and Neurology and a Distinguished Life Fellow of the American Psychiatric Association. He has presented papers at various conferences throughout the world including, "Biological, Psychological and Spiritual Perspectives in Psychiatry" and "The Medea Tragedy Updated." His publications include "Models of Madness: Science and Soul," in the Journal of Religion and Health, "The Insanity Defence, Revisited." in the Medico Legal Journal of Ireland, "The Many Faces of Faith," in the Journal of Ecumenical Studies, "Therapeutic Abortion, the Principle of Double Effect, and the Irish Compromise," in the Medico Legal Journal of Ireland and "The Concept of a Non Material Reality: Its Implications for Science and Religion," in CrossCurrents magazine. He is an emeritus faculty member of the Bible Studies program at St. Mary's Church in Lake Forest Illinois.

puisin9yr@aol.com

Joseph N. Goh is a Senior Lecturer in Gender Studies at the School of Arts and Social Sciences, Monash University Malaysia. He holds a PhD in gender, sexuality and theology, and his research interests include queer and LGBTI studies, human rights and sexual health issues, diverse theological and religious studies, and qualitative research. Goh is the author of numerous publications, including *Becoming a Malaysian Trans Man: Gender, Society, Body and Faith* (2020) and *Living Out Sexuality and Faith: Body Admissions of Malaysian Gay and Bisexual Men* (2018).

joseph.goh@monash.edu

Angelo Caranfa is emeritus scholar, who taught philosophy at Stonehill College, Easton, Massachusetts, and Bridgewater State College, at Bridgewater, Massachusetts. His areas of interest are twentieth-century French aesthetics and aesthetic education. His most recent publications have appeared in

CONTRIBUTORS

Philosophy and Theology, Educational Philosophy and Theory, Educational Theory, The Journal of Aesthetic Education, Journal of Philosophy of Education, Literature and Theology, The Journal of Art and Design Education, Soundings, and Art Criticism. In addition, he has published three books: Paul Claudel, Proust, and Camille Claudel.

caranfa@nextworlddesign.com

Alfredo Romagosa is the Director of Education of the Pedro Arrupe Jesuit Institute for Social Justice, and is an engineering consultant with Technology Base Corporation. He has degrees in Electrical Engineering from Marquette University, a Master of Science from the University of Miami, and a Master of Arts in Religious Studies from Barry University. He has taught computer science and theology courses at several universities. His current research interests are on Religion and Social Justice and Religion and Technology. Among his published articles are "St. Paul and the New Earth," "Teilhard, the Kingdom and the World," and "Integrated Data Management Tools for Real Time Applications." He holds two patents on computer design.

aromagosa@bellsouth.net

Bob Blundell is a freelance writer living in the Houston area. He has had fiction and creative non-fiction published in magazines such as The Bible Advocate, Liguorian, Dappled Things, Shattered, and Avalon Literary Review. He has also been a contributor to several of the *Divine Moments* book series.

bblun50@yahoo.com

Peter Heinegg was born in Brooklyn, spent seven years in Jesuit seminaries, received a B.A. in English from Fordham University and a Ph.D. in Comparative Literature from Harvard University. He has taught at Harvard, Queens College, C.U.N.Y and at Union College in Schenectady, where he is a professor of English and Comparative Literature. He is the author of numerous translations of books on religion and theology, of book reviews, and volumes of collected essays on religion and contemporary culture. He has contributed to the Christianity section of the Norton Anthology of World Religion. His special interests include the Bible, anti-Semitism, and the history of belief and unbelief in 19th century Europe.

peterheinegg@hotmail.com

For the history documents at the end of the issue:

chashenderson@mindspring.com

About the cover: Artwork on our anniversary issue cover was painted by Helene Masour

ymatusevich@alaska.edu

www.ingramcontent.com/pod-product-compliance
Lightning Source LLC
Chambersburg PA
CBHW040300170426
43193CB00020B/2955